SOVIET

MARKETING

SOVIET

MARKETING

Distribution in a Controlled Economy

MARSHALL I. GOLDMAN

The Free Press of Glencoe
Collier-Macmillan Ltd., London

ACKNOWLEDGMENTS

WITHOUT THE HELP and stimulation provided by various individuals, it seems certain that this book would never have been written. At the undergraduate level, Professor William N. Loucks of the University of Pennsylvania sparked my initial interest in the Soviet economy. At Harvard, Professor Alexander Gerschenkron encouraged me to proceed further than the Russian Area Program, my original goal. Entering the Economics Department, I continued my work under the guidance of Professor Abram Bergson. My work on the dissertation that served as the basis for this book was undertaken with the latter's advice and patient aid. I should also like to thank Robert Campbell, Nicholas DeWitt, Franklyn Holzman, Richard Judy, Basile Kerblay, and Herbert Levine. While others also deserve my thanks, it is to these colleagues that I am especially grateful.

Institutions and those associated with them have also been indispensable. The Russian Research Center with its library, working space, and stimulating associates is a unique place in the intellectual world. The help of the library staff in itself is something that cannot be repaid in any form of monetary compensation. Mrs. Helen Parsons, the executive secretary, and especially Marshall D. Shulman, the associate director, have provided understanding and aid when it was most needed. Mary Towle has done the typing for this project as well as for other papers of mine. The Harvard Business School and its International Marketing Institute are the other institutions which deserve my thanks. James Hagler, the executive director of the Institute, has made it possible for me to broaden my scope and direct my thoughts along broader comparative lines. Edward Bursk, the educational director of the Institute, is largely responsible for the publication of this manuscript. They were both responsible for interesting the Ford Foundation in the project, which in turn provided funds for me to visit the Soviet Union.

A word of thanks should also be given to those Soviet officials who have taken the trouble to receive me and explain various facets of their marketing system that no amount of descriptive reading could explain. While we have had disagreements and disputes, they have generally responded as scholars and friends. I hope this relationship will continue.

For the privilege of reprinting various portions of my articles, acknowledgment is made to the *Journal of Marketing,* national quarterly publication of the American Marketing Association, which printed, "Retailing in the Soviet Union," and "The Marketing Structure in the Soviet Union" from the April, 1960, and July, 1961, issues; to *Cahiers de L'institut de science economique appliquée,* which printed "Market Research for Consumer Goods in the United States and the Soviet Union," in May, 1961; to the *Quarterly Journal of Economics,* which printed "The Cost and Efficiency of Distribution in the Soviet Union" in August, 1962 (copyright, 1962, by The President and Fellows of Harvard College); and to the *Harvard Business*

Review, which published "Marketing—A Lesson for Marx," in January, 1960.

While they are neither colleagues nor directors of institutions, it is also necessary to express my appreciation to both my parents and my in-laws. All four have been patient and gracious during my prolonged gestation. Finally, of course, the one who deserves the most thanks of all is my wife. Not only has she read and reread every paper and chapter that I have ever written, but she has suggested improvements and pushed and shoved (although she has never kicked) me along the road to the completion of this book. In the final analysis, it is only a wife who can tolerate and understand the effort required. If for nothing else, for this she deserves my loving thanks.

MARSHALL I. GOLDMAN

Wellesley, Massachusetts
January, 1963

SPECIAL NOTE

All ruble amounts used in this book are in terms of the new 1961 ruble, which is equivalent to ten of the older rubles.

The abbreviation TsSU is used throughout for Tsentral'noe Statisticheskoe Upravlenie (The Central Statistical Administration).

CONTENTS

Acknowledgments *v*

1 Introduction *1*

2 The Organization of Soviet Domestic Trade *10*

3 Planning the Distribution of Consumer Goods *51*

4 Pricing of Consumers' Goods *83*

5 Financial Control *107*

6 The Human Element and State Ownership *129*

7 Costs of Distribution *151*

8 Marx, the U.S.S.R., and the Functions
   of Marketing *185*

Appendix: Historical Background *203*

Bibliography *209*

Index *225*

[1] *INTRODUCTION*

THE NATURE OF MARKETING

THE TRANSFER of goods from one person to another constituted one of man's earliest social acts. Whether the action was negotiated by means of force and violence or barter, man's inability to satisfy all his desires by producing everything himself has forced at least a partial reliance upon others for both necessities and luxuries. Initially this inability may have been due to weakness, but gradually with increased socialization, physical coercion became less important and increasingly the transfer of goods was marked by mutual exchange and trade.

The basic motive for trading is that somebody possesses something you desire more than something you have in your possession. By bringing such people into contact with one another, it is frequently possible to arrange a mutually satisfactory transaction. For the most part, therefore, trade is the exchange of surplus items for deficit items. Geographical and resource variations are one reason for surpluses. Among other factors are division of labor, variation

1

of skills, and differences in taste. One is led to create a surplus of some product in the hope that he may then bargain and exchange it for some other product for which he has a stronger desire.

As society and production grow in complexity and mass production and improved communications make it possible to expand the limits of the market, both the range of goods and the distance between negotiators increases. It becomes more and more difficult for the producers to locate one another and arrange mutually satisfactory exchanges between themselves without the aid of some sort of intermediary or middleman. The middleman, in this role of bringing together interested parties, has come to perform a variety of functions, which include buying, selling (which may involve advertising), transporting, storing, grading, financing, assembling, informing, bearing risk, packaging, refining, and altering the form of goods.

The nature of the contribution made by the middleman has long been a subject of controversy. While some functions (refining, packaging) are conceded to be completely productive in nature and others relatively productive (transporting and assembling), others are sometimes held to be parasitic (advertising, bearing risk, and, in some contexts, storing) to the basic processes of producing and consuming. Oddly enough, two of the most pronounced critics of these "parasitic" marketing practices have been the Catholic Church and the Marxists. Under the influence of Aristotle, the Church was opposed to anything or anybody who interposed himself between production and consumption and made a profit thereby. Undue transfers of title not affecting the nature of the goods themselves were felt to lead invariably to increases in price at the expense of both producers and consumers:

The essence of the argument was that payment may properly be demanded by the craftsmen who made the goods, for both labor in their vocation and serve the common need. The unpardonable sin is that of the speculator or the middle man who snatches private gain by the exploitation of private necessity (Tawney, 1926, p. 36).

Marx was similarly opposed to such "unproductive exploitation." Distribution activities were divided by him into two categories: "supplemental," those that were a continuation of the production process, and "pure," those that arose only because of the process of buying and selling (Marx, 1925, pp. 147–72). "Supplemental" production expenses were given the Marxian seal of approval. The cost of such activities, as determined by the labor expended, added to the value of the product. He included here such activities as packaging, storage, and transportation. It was assumed, of course, that no one was engaged in any of these practices in a socially unproductive manner, that is, by storing a good for an undue period of time merely to raise the price or by storing outmoded goods. In Marx's ideal society, such supplementary activities were really a continuation of the productive process. As a result, it was only natural that the value of labor expended in such work should normally be included in the final valuation of the commodity. If these same practices were undertaken in a capitalistic environment, however, the danger existed that the capitalist would use them to bring about an artificial price increase. Hence, even this potentially creative type of expense might not add to value as defined by Marx.

"Pure" costs of distribution were regarded by Marx as expenses arising solely because of a conversion of form (that is, the needless transfer of title among speculators, commission merchants, and others). Thus, as distinct from supplementary expenses, he felt that such costs could not add to the value of a good no matter how or when they were incurred. He considered all such merchandising activities to be uncreative. Essentially, anything more than simple retailing—that is advertising, operating commodity markets, speculating, carrying out commission activities, accounting, and so forth—was felt to be parasitic and of no value to society as a whole. "The general law is that *all expenses of circulation which arise only from changes of form do not add any value to the commodity*. They are merely expenses required for the realization of value or for its conversion from one form to another" (Marx, 1925, p. 169; italics in original).

Consequently, both the scholastics and the Marxists believed that elimination of pure costs of distribution and reduction of supplemental cost excesses would be in the best interests of society.

On the other hand, while modern Western authorities acknowledge that marketing has its excesses, it is generally asserted that a function is undertaken only if it performs a service and fulfills a need. This follows, they assert, because the act will not be carried out if it is unprofitable, and it will only be profitable if someone feels it provides a service worth the money. It is argued that almost all marketing activities do therefore contribute to the real value of a good, although there may be a difference between private and social value.

While it is difficult to assess the real contribution of certain marketing functions in any definitive manner, it may nevertheless be interesting to study an economic system in which there is the political power, as well as the ideological desire, to dispense with various "nonessential" functions. This may allow us to further our understanding of the nature and value of trade and to ascertain whether or not certain aspects of it can actually be eliminated. A study of the marketing operations in a country like the Soviet Union, where the marketing structure has such a different orientation, should prove valuable in illuminating the essence of the phenomenon.

THE AIMS OF THIS STUDY

The following examination of trade and distribution in the Soviet Union is thus undertaken for several reasons. On the one hand, this study may aid our understanding of the phenomenon of marketing. Even though there seems to be general agreement that trade is the one field of competition in which the West is safely ahead of the Russians and, therefore, about which we should know enough, there is still much we have to learn about the essence of marketing. If nothing else, we will be able to see ourselves and our activities better after subjecting someone else to examination.

On the other hand, any survey of the marketing process in the Soviet Union is highly desirable in itself. In the course of the last decade, Western economists have devoted considerable attention to many aspects of the economy of the Soviet Union. Economic investigations have ranged from the particular problem of transportation to the general problems of national income and growth. However, the area of domestic trade and distribution has been relatively neglected. Some earlier studies have been made, but the opportunity (one might say need) for research since 1953 has widened considerably.

The publication of detailed statistical handbooks and extensive descriptions of marketing operations enables the researcher to devote more time to analysis and less to detective work, thereby broadening his scope. At the same time, the extensive Soviet organizational changes and the increased concern with improvements in marketing following Stalin's death have all but necessitated a revision of the now outdated surveys of earlier years. Consequently, even if there were no implications in such a study for the basic marketing phenomenon, there nonetheless seems to be a need for an up-to-date survey of marketing in the Soviet Union.

Before outlining the structure of the monograph, something should be said regarding the limits of the proposed study. First, distribution is considered here only as it relates to the domestic sale of consumer goods, not to producers' goods or exports. Second, with minor exceptions, the basic production-goal decisions are assumed to be given. In the Soviet Union such goals are centrally determined by the policy makers, who steadfastly have emphasized heavy industry. Consequently, it is only within such circumscribed boundaries that the roles of consumer sovereignty, demand estimation, and product assortment are studied. The main concern here, then, is with the problems of allocating and delivering within the Soviet Union such goods as are produced. The establishment of basic production goals themselves is beyond the competence of this book.

THE STRUCTURE OF THIS STUDY

To provide the proper perspective, this book begins with a description of the organization of the distribution system in the Soviet Union. This, together with a brief historical appendix, furnishes the reader with a background for understanding the discussion that follows of some of the more challenging problems. The study then turns in Chapter 3 to an analysis of the trade-planning mechanism as it exists in theory and practice. For example, the ability to estimate the size of national purchasing power is found to be of little aid in ascertaining demand for a given item, in given sizes and styles, in given areas, at a given time of the year.

Chapter 4 considers the pricing procedures and the pricing interrelationships in a government-controlled society. What policies govern the establishment of the prices of consumers' goods? Following this, the system of financial controls and the methods by which the state attempts to regulate business operations through credit and banking restrictions are discussed in Chapter 5. The effectiveness of existing methods is analyzed, as well as pressures and counterpressures arising from the need to satisfy many goals. ·

Because the state is the owner of all property, from buildings and equipment to inventory on the shelf, marketing in the Soviet Union provides a good case study of the difficulties connected with delegating authority. Chapter 6 examines what happens when individuals are held responsible for state possessions and how the controls and checks that are adopted affect management, incentives, and service.

In an attempt to make some comparison of efficiency between the Soviet Union and the United States, the costs of distribution in the Soviet Union are analyzed (Chapter 7). The unusual Soviet definition of cost of distribution and its relationship to sales taxes and to markups has an effect on the level of distribution costs relative to sales. The chapter concludes with an examination of the significance of Soviet cost of distribution in connection with service and productivity.

The final chapter analyzes the newest directions in Soviet trade and the current emphasis on increased rationality. Increased reliance on the use of intermediaries between the producer and retailer and improvements in labor efficiency and capital utilization are characteristic of the most recent developments. The quest for increased rationality in the Soviet Union brings out hitherto neglected functions of the marketing phenomenon, which may be of special interest to Western economists. A major conclusion is that despite the waste connected with many marketing practices, certain basic functions seem to be essential. Regardless of the stage of economic development, and no matter what the prevalent political or religious doctrine, these functions cannot be eliminated if efficiency is to be maintained. Moreover, some of the marketing problems traditionally associated with highly developed "affluent" bourgeois societies also appear to be inevitable in less bourgeois but similarly highly developed conditions. As a bourgeois marketing economist has put it,

There is an old saying in marketing that "you can eliminate the middleman, but you cannot eliminate the functions he performs." Consequently, omitting a middleman may or may not reduce marketing costs. If that middleman is performing economically a necessary function, his removal will mean that someone else must now perform that function, with the result that the marketing costs will not be reduced. In fact, if the new performer is not so efficient as the former one, the cost may even be increased (Phillips and Duncan, 1956, p. 32).

[2] *THE ORGANIZATION OF SOVIET DOMESTIC TRADE*

INTRODUCTION

THE SIMPLE but perplexing question of how goods reach the Soviet consumer is an elementary, but inadequately understood, matter in the West. This chapter will describe the main channels and the administrative apparatus that exist for the distribution of consumers' goods in the Soviet Union.

To provide perspective, it may help to sketch briefly the distribution procedure in the United States. While there are numerous exceptions, the basic distribution pattern of consumers' goods in our country is from factory to wholesaling agency to retailer to consumer. Some variations include the direct sale of goods from factory to retailer (a dress manufacturer), the wholesale transfer of items by a subsidiary of the manufacturer (a large electrical appliance manufacturer) or of the retailer (a grocery chain), or the performance of all functions from manufacturing to retailing by one organization (a mail order house). Generally, however, orders and sales estimates originate at the retail level and goods are passed to the lower echelons with almost no intervention by governmental agencies.

An outline of the distribution channels in the Soviet Union is somewhat similar. As in the United States, the pattern of Soviet distribution is from factory to wholesaler to retailer to consumer. There are major differences, however. Normally the Russian wholesale and retail organizations are not independent of one another but are controlled by the same parent organization. For the most part, the manufacturing enterprises are under the jurisdiction of unrelated government organizations, although occasionally, as in the United States, there may be direct selling from factory to retailer, as well as common control of all three links. In the latter case, the manufacturing link is usually little more than a workshop. The most important difference, of course, is that the role of government is much larger in the Soviet Union. The state not only owns all the trading facilities, but it administers and controls distribution, functionally at the wholesale stage and geographically at the local, regional, and republic levels.

There are two main trade networks in the Soviet Union. The government store network is the largest and is located exclusively in urban areas. The cooperative store network consists primarily of rural outlets with some city branches. Both networks have their own wholesale and supply systems. A third minor type of outlet located in both rural and urban areas is the *kolkhoz* (collective farm) market. The latter has no formal wholesale or supply system and is administered through the government store administrative hierarchy. The sales volume of each network is presented in Table 1.

Table 1—Retail Sales Volume by Trade Network
(in Million Rubles, Prices of Respective Year)

Year	Government Trade	Cooperative Trade	Commission Trade	Total (1), (2), & (3)	Private Trade	Total (4) & (5)
	(1)	(2)	(3)	(4)	(5)	(6)
1924	99	186		285	319	605
1925	160	352		512	386	898
1926	215	546		761	521	1,282
1927	233	706		939	496	1,435
1928	250	927		1,177	364	1,541
1929	334	1,186		1,520	243	1,763
1930	448	1,445		1,893	112	2,006
1931	726	2,068		2,794		
					Kolkhoz market	
1932	1,445	2,581		4,036	750	4,786
1933	2,512	2,467		4,979	1,150	6,129
1934	3,682	2,499		6,181	1,400	7,581
1935	6,315	1,856		8,171	1,450	9,621
1936	7,981	2,695		10,676	1,560	12,236
1937	9,285	3,309		12,594	1,780	14,374
1938	9,988	4,014		14,002	2,440	16,442
1939	11,606	4,977		16,583	2,990	19,573
1940	12,808	4,700		17,508	2,910	20,418
1941				15,280		
1942				7,780		
1943				8,400		
1944				11,930		
1945	12,460	3,554		16,014	13,640	29,654
1946	19,853	4,870		24,723		
1947	25,174	7,906		33,080		
1948	23,248	7,775		31,023		
1949	24,286	9,225		33,511	4,570	38,081
1950	26,104	9,854		35,958	4,920	40,878
1951	27,401	10,584		37,985	5,080	43,065
1952	28,489	10,870		39,359	5,370	44,729
1953	30,868	12,196	7	43,071	4,880	47,951
1954	33,565	14,399	224	48,188	4,900	53,088
1955	34,736	14,968	490	50,194	4,782	54,976
1956	38,062	16,016	665–704	54,743	4,210	58,953
1957	43,296	18,432	773–823	62,501	3,960	66,461
1958	46,794	20,055	871–939	67,720	4,050	71,770
1959	49,807	21,244	872–950	71,923	3,831	75,754
1960	54,904	22,906	745–795	78,555	3,604	82,159
1961	56,800	23,400	847	81,000		

SOURCE: TsSU 3, pp. 740-41, 787; TsSU 5, pp. 673, 681, 696, 736; TsSU 6, pp. 14, 16, 19, 20; TsSU 8, p. 425. Lifits 1950, pp. 11, 236, 317; 1955, p. 85. Dadugin and Fedorov, 1957, pp. 9, 12. TsSU 13, p. 356; Pravda, Jan. 23, 1962.

GOVERNMENT STORE NETWORK

Retail Outlets

The sale of nonfood goods in the government store network will be considered first. The Soviet urban consumer has a relatively wide selection of stores in which to shop. There are specialized stores (*spetsializirovannye magaziny*) that sell only a particular type of goods such as clothing, as well as the department stores that provide an assortment of various goods. By far the largest and finest stores are in the center of the large cities, especially such Moscow department stores as GUM (*Glavnyi Universalnyi Magazin,* or *Univermag*) with a staff of 4,300 and TsUM (*Tsentralnyi Univermag*) with 2,300 employees, and the Leningrad department stores *Gorodskoi Passazh* and *Dom Leningradskaia Torgovlia* with staffs of over 900 each (TsSU 7, p. 101). Reconstruction of Leningrad's *Gostinyi Dvor* will be completed before 1965, making it the largest department store in the Soviet Union. Another type of department store different from anything in the West is the relatively new *Detskii Mir,* Children's World. It is a new and large specialized department store devoted entirely to children. With a staff of 3,200, it combines the sale of toys and clothes with almost all other children's products from toiletries to furniture.

The neighborhood outlets of the specialized stores are often located on the street floor of the larger multistory apartment house units. Moreover, there are a few department stores in residential neighborhoods, such as *Dzerzhin-*

skii Univermag in Moscow, and the *Kirovskii* and the *Frunzenskii Univermagy* in Leningrad.

When shopping for groceries, the Soviet urban consumer may also select from a wide variety of government stores. The central city placement of the largest and most spectacular food stores in Russia contrasts sharply with the United States and its automobile-oriented outlying supermarkets. In the Soviet Union, the locational pattern of food stores is very similar to that of other stores, with the largest stores in the center of the city.

The largest and best multiproduct grocery stores in Russia are called *Gastronomy*. Appropriately enough, one of the largest occupies the first floor of GUM. There is also a wide selection of specialized stores—dairies, meat markets, bakeries, vegetable shops, and delicatessens—in which to shop. Usually the housewife can find a wider selection of a given specialty in these shops than in the traditionally smaller all-purpose grocery store (*prodmag*), which resembles what is known in the United States as the "corner" grocery store. In any event, the size of the typical food outlet, specialized or unspecialized, is relatively small, with only one or two sales clerks.

Reversing an earlier trend, Russian marketing officials in 1955 began to emphasize the specialized type of outlet. By 1960, specialized food shops constituted 44 per cent of all urban food stores in the Soviet Union. Russian marketing experts argue that increased specialization not only provides the Soviet consumer with a wider selection of goods but improves services and labor productivity and decreases costs of distribution (Serebriakov, 1956, p. 50).

Restaurants

Worthy of a paper devoted entirely to their organization and problems, city restaurants in the Soviet Union—including everything from milk bars and tea shops to exclusive hotel restaurants—are also considered to be government stores. As of January 1, 1961, there were 108,800 such eating places in the urban areas of the Soviet Union. Total urban restaurant sales amounted to 6 billion rubles in 1960 or 10 per cent of total urban sales (TsSU 5, pp. 683, 722).

Other Government Stores

The preceding section has described the trade network of the Ministry of Trade, the largest component of what is usually referred to as the urban government store system. Within the general category of government stores, however, there are some special organizations that deal with both food and nonfood items.

In numbers almost as large as the official Ministry of Trade network but much less significant in terms of sales volume, the Workers Supply Departments (*otdely rabochegosnabzheniia*, ORS), are a peculiar Soviet institution. Although they are administratively classed as government stores, their closest counterpart in the United States is the factory cafeteria. There is a considerable difference, however, between an American factory cafeteria and the ORS. In addition to the provision of food and meals, the latter sells nonfood consumers' goods, although food sales and meals are relatively more important. Quality and price are usually better than average, especially for industrially processed items. The supplies are often provided from the factory's own farm or vegetable plots, a questionable division of labor.

The ORS are also comparable to the United States military Post Exchanges, which sell manufactured goods and meals to military personnel. However, since there is also a Post Exchange system for military personnel in the Soviet Union, it may not be wise to make too much of this analogy. Information about Soviet military Post Exchanges is not plentiful, but one of the largest Moscow department stores, the central department store of the Ministry of Defense of the USSR, had 563 employees as of 1957 and a sales volume about half that of the *Gorodskoi Passazh* department store in Leningrad.

Outlets selling drugs, periodicals, and books are classed as government stores but are not supervised by the Ministry of Trade. The drugstores are the most important of these outlets. The Ministry of Health operates over 7,000 drugstores (*magaziny*) and over 4,000 smaller outlets (*palatki*) in the RSFSR (Russian Socialist Federated Soviet Republic). The distribution of periodicals is the responsibility of the Ministry of Communication. Although there are few stores, there are over 6,000 newspaper stands in the RSFSR. Books are sold through the bookstore network of the Ministry of Culture. Recently many of their outlets were transferred to the complete control of either the Ministry of Trade or the cooperative societies. In 1957, for example, most of the rural bookstores were merged into the cooperative trade network.

There are other miscellaneous government enterprises. They include pawnshops (*lombard*), secondhand shops (*skupochnye magaziny*), and commission trade stores for industrial goods, where personal possessions and handicraft items may be resold for a commission by the state. However, the Ministry of Trade network, the ORS, the special ministry stores, and the restaurants essentially constitute the government store network. It is in these 370,000 outlets that the Soviet urban consumers do virtually all their shopping and eating.

Shopping in Soviet Stores

Since the ritual of shopping is somewhat different in the Soviet Union than it is in the United States, it may be worth while to describe a typical transaction. The first thing to be noted is that Soviet stores are open on Sundays and on most secular holidays, when the factory workers are free and able to shop; most retail stores are thus closed Mondays and the day after any holiday.

Upon entering the store, the customer typically finds a line of people before him. In due time, it is his turn for service. Often with a cold unsolicitous tone, the salesclerk inquires of the shopper's needs. If the customer finds something that suits him, all he can do at this stage is to ask the price and permission to examine the goods. He then leaves the salesclerk (without the merchandise) and enters a new line in front of the cashier (*kassa*). Here he pays the cashier the ruble amount of the price just quoted to him by the salesclerk, and, in return, receives a receipt (*chek*). With his receipt in hand, the shopper moves to a third line. After turning in his receipt to the *kontroler*, he finally receives his package. Unless the typically crowded Russian store is empty, this means he has had to queue up three times before being able to walk out with his purchase. The Russians call this the "*kassa* system."

Clearly the *kassa* system has been costly in terms of

both time and money. To expedite the purchasing routine, a number of so-called progressive methods of trade have been introduced. The first to be considered is *bez prodavtsa*, literally, service without the aid of salesclerks. The temptation is to describe this as self-service, but it is not the same. The Russian version of sales without a salesclerk means that when the customer enters the store, he need not stand in line to ask the salesclerk what is available and the price; instead, the goods and their prices are displayed on the wall or in glass cases. The customer can therefore walk in, choose an item, and find its cost without having to wait in line. He must still stand in two queues, however, to pay the cashier and to pick up his goods. The goods he examines are locked in the cases or securely anchored. There have been one or two experiments in which the salesclerks have been allowed to receive cash and personally hand over the goods, but this has not been widespread and usually is permitted for items of very small cost only.

Self-service (*samo obsluzhivaniia*) as it is known in the West is a relatively new phenomenon in the Soviet Union. It was first introduced in late 1954 by a Leningrad food store. Although it has been widely adopted in the selling of food, it is also being used in other outlets. As of January, 1961, there were approximately 8,500 self-service stores in operation throughout the country.

On entering a store, the customer must first check all his parcels. While this inconvenience seems bothersome enough, at one time there were even more obstacles confronting the Soviet consumer. Initially, only a few customers were allowed into the store at a time—mainly in order to prevent shoplifting. Consequently, as late as July, 1957, there were complaints published about the long lines outside the stores and the fact that often there were as many store personnel inside as customers.

Having passed all the entrance requirements, the customer is then able to select his groceries and place them either in a little handbasket, often provided by the store, or in a little handbag carried by most Soviet shoppers. A few stores have the customary Western carts, but this seems a little too costly, especially in retail trade, where capital is scarce. Because of their showpiece nature, commodity selection in the supermarkets is fairly wide, and the newer stores may even have open refrigrated cabinets. Most of the stores, however, still have a poor assortment of products.

With his selection completed, the shopper moves to the checkout counter. Originally he first had to go to a *kontroler,* who computed the total of the purchases. Then, following the same old scheme, he went to the cashier to pay and receive a receipt; and only then could he return to the *kontroler* and walk out with the goods and the parcels previously checked.

It was soon discovered that only one person, the *kontroler-cashier,* was needed to determine the total and collect the money. The calculation of the total cost of the purchases is made on an abacus and the result entered on a cash register. As yet the Russians do not have many cash registers that also add. Although some stores still retain an additional *kontroler* at the exit to insure that packages and checked parcels belong to the proper person, the overall operation of self-service—especially its more recent improvements—is more satisfactory and efficient than the older method.

In addition to the improved sales procedures, several other innovations have been introduced. A state mail-order service, *Posyltorg,* was formed a few years ago and now has an annual sales volume of approximately 100 million rubles. A Soviet citizen can order any one of 5,000 articles from a ninety-nine-page illustrated catalog. Vending machines for soft drinks, milk, beer, sandwiches, and hard goods have now become commonplace throughout the Soviet Union. A machine has been developed that sprays essence of Soviet cologne over the consumer's hair for a few kopecks. Operational problems are many, however, and, aside from complaints about the unprofitable location of various machines, the service is poor and the machines are often inadequately supplied. It is not an uncommon sight to see a row of soda-pop vending machines adjacent to a woman vendor selling the same thing from her portable stand. In some instances, the vendor is not just adjacent to the vending machines but in front of them.

Administrative Organization
of the Government Store Network

Having described the various retail outlets and services in the government store network, it is now necessary to sketch the structure of the internal organization of the stores and the organization of their senior administrative units. The principles of organization are somewhat similar to those prevailing in many American firms with a three-way division of personnel into administration, operations, and service.

At the retail level in the Soviet Union, the administrative functions are performed by the manager, who may have several assistants, depending on the size of the store. They in turn direct the *tovarovedy,* the heads of the various store departments and sections. The manager's staff also includes a planning and accounting section made up of the chief bookkeeper, accountants, planners, and statisticians. The last two are more likely to be absent from the typical staff in a capitalist country. Secretaries and office help are also included under the administrative section.

The second and largest group consists of operating personnel, and includes the cashiers, controllers, and sales-clerks, who are ranked according to training and experience. Supplemental trade personnel—packers, checkers, clerks, storehouse employees, and decorators—are included in this group as a subcategory.

The third classification, service personnel, includes among others the janitors, guards, machinists, electricians, and repairmen. In addition, many retail outlets have their own subsidiary branches that repair, and on occasion produce, goods. These workers are considered to be either service or productive personnel.

Of course, not all stores are large enough to warrant such a division of labor. In the smaller stores there may be a manager and another salesclerk, although generally a salesclerk force of three per working shift is typical. The number of salesclerks depends on the space available in a store as well as the store hours and the number of working shifts. Traditionally, the salesclerk is assigned to a given counter area (*rabochii mest*), although a more recent practice is to assign a group of salesclerks to a section of the store, thereby increasing the mobility of personnel.

At the next higher stage, the organizational chart varies depending on the size and location of the stores to be administered. If they are large enough, stores may report directly to an administrative agency operating at the republic level. Typically, however, the average government store is under the control of the local city trade organization called a *torg*. As of January, 1957, there were 971 *torgi* and 293 affiliates (Gogol', 1958 p. 44).

Generally, each city has its own trade organization, depending on the size of the city and the area in which the city is located. The larger, as well as the more remote, cities have organizations that tend to be more specialized and independent. The cities of Moscow, Leningrad, Kiev, Sverdlosk, and Baku, for example, have separate *torgi* for food and manufactured goods; and some, especially Moscow, have specialized *torgi* for various kinds of industrial goods.

The functions of such units include the administration and operation of all the retail outlets within their jurisdiction, as well as the operation of some wholesale facilities. The trade organization, or *torg*, also provides certain services for its stores. It is somewhat comparable to the "unit" in the centralized chain of command of the Great Atlantic & Pacific Tea Company, with the slight difference that all the stores in an area, not just the food outlets, would belong to the A & P.

A typical *torg* is headed by a director with a small personal staff including a lawyer and a health inspector. The main body of the *torg* is composed of trade departments (*otdel*) with a buyer (*tovaroved*) in charge of each department. They order and supply goods for the whole city, and supervise and inspect the operation of the subordinate retail operation itself. The warehouses (*sklady* and *bazy*) attached to the *torg* are also supervised by the buyers. If the *torg* is big enough, there is a special department for economic planning (market research and plan formation) consisting of an economist, a planner, and a statistician. This department may be entirely separate from the bookkeeping staff, which is responsible for accounting, financial

inventory, and control matters. Plant and equipment supervision is the responsibility of the maintenance department.
Depending on the scope of operations, other departments
may be established to supervise personnel, restaurants, and
the operation of subsidiary production units. This is usually
the case as one moves along the chain of command to
higher trade organizations at the *oblast* or *krai* (state or
county) level.

Above this structure is the Republic Ministry of Trade,
which has much the same framework as the subordinate
units under its jurisdiction. Since the Ministry of Trade
also performs administrative, operational, and service functions, it too tends to classify its work into such organizational divisions. The organizational composition of the
Ministry of Trade of the RSFSR as of January, 1959, is a
typical example of how administrative supervision is combined with operational and service functions at the republic
levels. (See Table 2.)

Table 2—Organization of the Ministry of Trade RSFSR, January, 1959

A. Administration and control
  1. Administration *(Upravlenie)* of: Food sales, bakery product sales, manu-
     factured goods, restaurants, planning economic commission, organization
     of trade, technology and capital construction, cadres.
  2. Department *(Otdel)* of: Pricing, labor and wages, productive enterprises,
     transportation, finance, legal matters, accounting, complaint bureau.
  3. Main Administration *(Glavnoe Upravlenie)* of: Inspection, resort areas,
     Far North, material technical supply *(Glavsnab)*.
B. Operational and wholesaling (offices and warehouses)
  1. Office *(Kontor)* of: *Rosmiasorybtorg* (meats, fats, fish), *rosbakaleia* (grocer-
     ies), *rostekstiltorg* (textiles), *rostorgodezhda* (clothes), *rosobuvtorg* (shoes),
     roskhoztorg (household goods), *roskulttorg* (cultural and sporting goods),
     rosgalantereia (haberdashery, toiletries, cosmetics, perfumes), *roslesstroi-
     torg* (lumber and construction material), *rosiuvelirtorg* (jewelry).
C. Functional services
  1. *Posyltorg* (mail order).

2. *Torgposredkontora* (Commission Agent Office—Trade Fairs).
3. *Rostorgmontazh* (refrigeration operation and service).
4. *Rostorgstroi* (construction and repair).
5. *Torgreklama* (advertising offices).
6. NITTOP (Institute for Scientific Research of Store and Restaurant Operation).

SOURCE: *Sovetskaia Torgovlia,* Jan. 8, 1959, p. 4.

Administrative offices (*upravlenie*) in the Ministry of Trade administer the various types of stores in the republic. For example, the Administration for Food Products exercises control vertically over food stores throughout the republic. There are also administrations for the supervision of stores selling bakery and manufactured goods. This is in addition to the control extended horizontally by the trade organizations in the cities.

There are other marketing activities and functions over which the Ministry of Trade has ultimate administrative authority. Almost all of the administrative tasks of the various lower-echelon units are performed on a somewhat grander scale by agencies of the ministry. What may be an administrative detail that a clerk can solve in the city trade organization becomes an important policy matter for a specialized administration at the apex of the organizational pyramid. Thus, there are administrations in the Ministry of Trade for planning and allocating sales volume, for technology, for capital construction, for personnel, and for training and education. There are also departments concerned with administering wages, prices, subsidiary production organizations, transportation, finance and legal arbitration, bookkeeping, store maintenance and quality inspection throughout the system.

The main operational activity of the Ministry of Trade is wholesaling. As mentioned earlier, wholesaling is also an operational function of agencies other than those attached directly to the Ministry of Trade. Many of the local trade organizations (*torgi*) operate their own warehouses and perform a wholesaling function for stores directly under their supervision. Nonetheless, the major responsibility for the wholesaling operation belongs to the Ministry of Trade. Sixty per cent of all the wholesaling in the Russian Republic (RSFSR) is carried out by offices of the Ministry of Trade. Sales offices of the State Planning Commission (Gosplan), the regional economic councils (*sovnarkhozy*), the consumer cooperatives, and the Ministries of Health and Communication handle the rest (Serebrennikov, Oct., 1960, p. 7).

There are two types of wholesale units: the *vykhodnaia baza* and the *torgovlaia baza*. The first is the warehouse attached to the factory and is the shipping base. The second is an intermediate receiving warehouse that may deliver directly to a store or a retail warehouse (*torgovlyi sklad*). Depending on the size of the warehouse (*baza*) and the volume of business, the administrative unit controlling the warehouse is either an office (*kontor*) or an administration (*upravlenie*). The administration is the larger and more important of the two.

Although recently the emphasis has been on decentralization and horizontal interaction, the normal chain of command in wholesaling and administration continues to rise vertically. Depending on the nature of the goods, the local offices are controlled by republic-level offices that are directly subordinate to the republic Minister of Trade. Each chain of offices is responsible for the wholesale distribution of a certain class of commodities. For instance, the shoe office in the Ministry of Trade supervises the activities of its subordinate offices as they receive shoes from the manufacturers and ship them to trade organizations throughout the country.

In addition to these administrative and operational activities, agencies of the Ministry of Trade perform certain service functions. For example, units of the ministry also service refrigerated equipment and handle construction and repair problems. The Ministry of Trade of the RSFSR also has responsibility for the various marketing institutes and schools, such as the Plekhanov Institute in Moscow and the Frederick Engels Institute in Leningrad.

Within the last few years the nature of some of the ministry's activities has changed. As indicated in Table 2 the Ministry of Trade now includes an advertising office. As the stores and city trade organizations started to form their own advertising offices, duplication of effort became a serious problem. To bring about the consolidation of advertising activity, Torgreklama, an advertising agency at the republic level, was formed in late 1958. As part of the Ministry of Trade of the RSFSR, the agency's director, T. S. Stepaniants, in effect was given power to establish advertising policy for the whole USSR. By 1961, there were agencies in most major Soviet cities as well as coordinating agencies for almost all the Soviet republics.

· The functions of Soviet advertising agencies are both narrower and broader than the functions of similar agencies in the United States. On the one hand, Russian agencies generally restrict themselves to problems of advertising and do not concern themselves with market research, new products, and improved marketing methods. These special functions are the responsibility of NITTOP, the Institute for Scientific Research of Store and Restaurant Operation, a companion organization in the Ministry of Trade. On the other hand, since the government owns all marketing facilities in the country, including advertising agencies, the Russian agencies perform certain services that in this country might be undertaken by the American Marketing Association or by trade associations. Torgreklama (the advertising agency of the RSFSR) is responsible for the content of the advertising courses that are taught in the institutes and of the textbooks and bulletins that are published by the Ministry of Trade. Such varied activities as advertising contests and national and international advertising conferences are also under the jurisdiction of Torgreklama.

In addition to this type of activity, there are the normal direct advertising duties. For a commission, Torgreklama, or any city agency, will prepare advertising copy for magazines, posters, and billboards, as well as commercials for radio and television. Advertisements for local and provincial newspapers will also be created. (Only *Pravda* and *Izvestiia* do not carry ads.) The advertising agency of the Ukraine (Ukrtorgreklama) even puts out a special evening paper, *Vechernogo Kieva,* which contains news and shopping hints for the citizens of Kiev.

In conjunction with the Ministry of Culture, the republic trade agencies also prepare advertising filmstrips for presentation both in movie theatres and over television. In 1960, fifteen such filmstrips in the RSFSR were prepared and reportedly were seen by fifty million people. It was anticipated that fifty-two such films would be made in 1961.

Information on advertising fees in the Soviet Union is rather limited. An approximation of specific media fees was given to this author by the director of Torgreklama, Mr. Stepaniants. An advertisement (no indication as to size of ad) in an all-Union newspaper costs 200 to 350 rubles (approximately $200 to $380). If an ad is placed in a provincial newspaper, it costs only 80 to 120 rubles. Advertising on the radio is much cheaper; a minute and a half on an all-Union network costs between 50 and 60 rubles. Television is even less expensive; a minute of time on television can be obtained for 21 rubles. The reason given for the lower television rate is that television is seen only in several cities.

Integration of Trade Organizations with the Government

As the peak of the administrative pyramid in the Ministry of Trade is reached, the proportion of effort and staff devoted to purely administrative and bureaucratic functions steadily increases. This is not much different from the organizational make-up of any large multistage corporation in the West. Furthermore, the traditional organizational pattern in Russia is about the same as in other countries; the three-way division of activity into administration, operation, and service seems to have been a convenient one. The major difference between the organizational structures of Soviet and Western marketing operations is the complete integration of Soviet marketing activities into the normal body of state organizations.

The chief officials of the trade organizations serve as the commercial representatives in the regular governmental body at each administrative level. The city trade organization is represented by its director on the municipal council or city soviet. Trade officials also participate in the general governmental administrative and control organs that exist at the county and state (*krai* and *oblast*) level. In recent years, however, some of the power that the state government organizations have had over trade matters has been transferred to the regional economic council (*sovnarkhoz*). Although it is primarily concerned with industrial production, the *sovnarkhoz* through its trade committee seems to have taken a larger role in the operation of trade within its jurisdiction. This may eventually result in a closer link between productive and distributive agencies.

The ultimate in the governmental framework is, of course, the Council of Ministers, first at the republic level and then at the all-Union level. As was true of the trade organizations at the lower levels, the Ministry of Trade of the various republics is the unit responsible for everything relating to consumer trade within the republic. It is through the Minister of Trade that the Council of Ministers (which includes the Minister of Trade) regulates marketing activity. The Council of Ministers issues orders and delegates authority to the Ministry of Trade, which in turn carries out the orders, exercises authority, and provides the Council with the material it needs for decision-making.

Until November, 1958, the organizational pyramid described above, and shown in Figure 1, extended to the all-Union level. The Ministry of Trade of the USSR coordinated the work of all the subordinate republic ministries, including that of the largest—the Russian Republic (RSFSR). Its structure was almost the exact duplicate of the present Ministry of Trade of the Russian Republic. In fact, even the personnel was much the same. Dmitri Pavlov, who is now the Minister of Trade of the RSFSR, was Minister of Trade of the USSR.

As part of the over-all trend toward Soviet decentralization, which took place in the late 1950's, the all-Union

Figure 1—Traditional Chain of Command in Trade until Late 1958

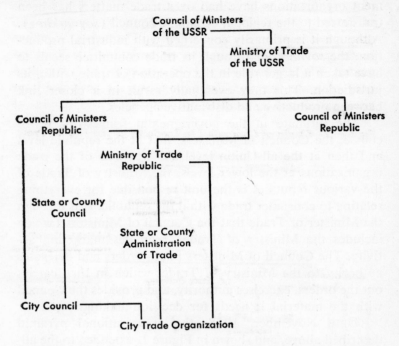

Ministry of Trade was abolished on November 27, 1958. Wherever possible, the activities of the Ministry of Trade of the USSR were shifted to the republic level (intrarepublic wholesaling, allocation of locally produced goods, price formation, quality inspection, education, personnel and so forth). Obviously there were many activities that could not be transferred in this fashion. For example the task of coordinating and directing interrepublic or all-Union trade could not be undertaken by a republic Ministry, nor were such functions abolished. Although the Ministry of

Trade of the USSR is gone, its functions are still performed.

To cope with interrepublic problems, many of the tasks of an all-Union nature formerly performed by the Ministry of Trade of the USSR have been assigned to the state planning commission (Gosplan, USSR). The role of Gosplan in the planning and operation of marketing has been extended. While it has always been concerned with the planning of trade, for the first time Gosplan's activities have been broadened to include not only the establishment of

Figure 2—Chain of Command in Trade as of the Fall of 1960

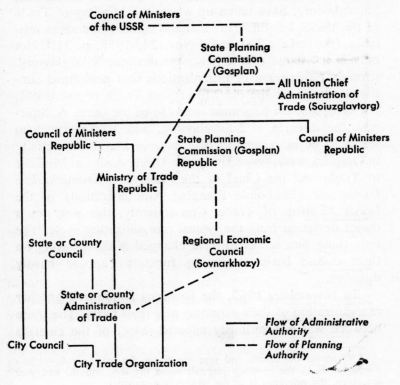

planned retail sales but also the distribution of funded (physically allocated) goods and the setting of retail and wholesale prices for certain important consumers' goods traded on an interrepublic basis. A newly created organization, Soiuzglavtorg (all-Union Chief Administration of Trade) implements many of the decisions of Gosplan, its parent, and also makes similar allocation and delivery decisions for goods of a lower priority traded on an interrepublic basis. Figure 2 outlines the table of organization in trade as of the fall of 1960.

It would seem, therefore, that Gosplan and its affiliate, Soiuzglavtorg, have taken up where the Ministry of Trade of the USSR left off. This includes making the same mistakes (*Sovetskaia Torgovlia,* Nov. 24, 1959, p. 3).* Not only is the name of the new organization, Soiuzglavtorg, strongly reminiscent of organizations that performed similar duties under the old Ministry of Trade of the USSR, but here, too, the personnel seems to be the same. A. Smirnov, the director of Soiuzglavtorg, and V. Tiukov, who seems to be in command of consumer marketing activity in Gosplan, were, respectively, the USSR Assistant Minister of Trade and the Chief of the *Planovo-Ekonomicheskoe Upravlenie* (Economic Planning Administration) of the USSR Ministry of Trade. Consequently, this was not a major deviation from the typical reorganization cycle. The only thing that seems to have changed is the lettering on their doors; basic marketing functions appear hardly different.

In November, 1962, the Russians announced another reorganization of their economy and their party. The trade network was not seriously affected. Most of the changes

---

* Whenever the month and year are given, the reference *Sovetskaia Torgovlia,* is to the monthly journal; when the *day,* month, and year are given, the reference is to the triweekly newspaper.

were at the general planning level and affected industrial planning. In the marketing structure, only those organizations linking the trade organizations with the Council of Ministers were altered. (See Figure 2a.)

These changes in both 1958 and 1962 would seem to support an observation that will be noted again. Once the state undertakes the conduct of domestic trade, it may shift

Figure 2a—Chain of Command in Trade as of November 1962

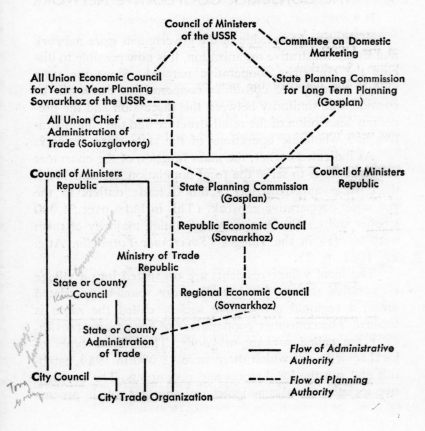

Council of Ministers of the USSR

Committee on Domestic Marketing

All Union Economic Council for Year to Year Planning Sovnarkhoz of the USSR

State Planning Commission for Long Term Planning (Gosplan)

All Union Chief Administration of Trade (Soiuzglavtorg)

Council of Ministers Republic

State Planning Commission (Gosplan)

Council of Ministers Republic

Republic Economic Council (Sovnarkhoz)

Ministry of Trade Republic

State or County Council

Regional Economic Council (Sovnarkhoz)

State or County Administration of Trade

City Council

City Trade Organization

———— Flow of Administrative Authority

- - - - Flow of Planning Authority

the various functions around among multi-titled institutions, but it cannot eliminate any basic functions regardless of the ideological implications. A comparison of Figure 1 with Figures 2 and 2a may help to illustrate this point. (See Appendix.)

THE CONSUMER COOPERATIVE NETWORK

With some knowledge of the government store network and its administrative organization, it is now possible to discuss the consumer cooperative network. Since the state closely controls the consumer cooperatives, there will be considerable similarity between this discussion and the preceding description of the retail structure and the administrative and wholesale operations of the state store network.

As indicated earlier, the main function of the consumer cooperatives is to serve the rural population. By mid-1962, there were approximately 326,000 trade outlets in the consumer cooperative network. (This includes over 51,000 smaller stalls.) By far the overwhelming majority of them were located in the villages (*Sovetskaia Torgovlia,* Aug. 23, 1962, p. 2).

The local village residents are organized into a village cooperative society (*sel'po*). In more sparsely populated areas, a regional cooperative society called the *raipo* is formed. The consumer cooperatives of state farms (*sovkhozy*) are called *sovkhoz-rabkoopy.* These three types of local societies, of which there were 18,000 in 1959, establish and run the local stores and restaurants. The cooperative societies are also assigned an important role in procuring agricultural produce from the *kolkhozy*, especially in remote areas where it is not feasible for government procurement agencies to operate. Although the number of outlets has increased, the number of societies has diminished from 28,000 in 1947 to 18,000 in 1961, largely as a result of the consolidation of many of the *kolkhozy* and the development of the virgin land areas. Furthermore, this development explains why the number of stockholders ceased to fall and began to increase after 1952. From a peak in 1947 of 36 million, membership fell to 32 million; by 1962 it had risen to more than 43 million.

The typical village shop (*sel'skaia lavka*) resembles our small general store. It provides staple foods, such as salt, and manufactured items, such as soap, matches, and cigarettes. Frequently such shops are only a room in someone's home (Serebriakov, 1956, p. 66n). As of January 1, 1958, there were approximately 171,600 such outlets with an average of 1.14 salesclerk's positions (*rabochii mest*) (*Vestnik Statistiki*, No. 8, 1958, p. 91). Serving several smaller areas and a larger population, the next larger type of outlet (*sel'mag*) offers a wider selection of manufactured goods. The consumer society (*sel'po*) supervises both types of shops. With a large enough market, a given society may actually run several shops. There were approximately 28,000 such shops in January, 1958, with an average of 1.84 salesclerk's positions.

In the rural regional centers and in areas of population growth, stores for specialized food and industrial goods may be opened. At the beginning of 1958 there were about 28,300 such stores, including small department stores; shops for clothing, shoes, and books; and outlets for household goods and construction materials. It is also possible for the rural resident to place mail orders through the government mail-order organization, Posyltorg. In late 1959, the consumer cooperative system opened up its own mail-order service designed especially for members in the virgin land areas.

One of the best methods to illustrate the unusual characteristics of Soviet consumer cooperatives is to compare them with Western consumer cooperatives that have been patterned after the Rochdale model. Many students, as well as professional marketing authorities, are confused by the semantics of the situation and have been led to believe that the Soviet cooperatives are no different from the Rochdale model.

One difference that we have already noted is that the consumer cooperatives in the Soviet Union have generally been restricted to the village. Western consumer cooperatives are subject to no such restraint. Moreover, members of cooperative societies in the West, while encouraged to patronize the cooperatives, have alternative outlets nearby from which to choose. In the Soviet Union, the only escape from the monopoly control of the cooperatives in rural areas is a government store located in the city. Even though over 20 per cent of the cash purchases of the peasants are made in urban areas, this is not the type of competitive stimulus normally faced by a cooperative organization in the West. If anything, it may indicate the unavailability of certain goods in the rural areas.

Because they are said to be self-governing, the 42 million shareholders (*chlenov-paischikov*) are supposed to hold local meetings not less than twice a year, vote dues, and elect (1) a governing board *(pravlenie)*, (2) the director, (3) an inspection committee (*revizionnaia komissiia*) to check the economic and financial activities of the governing board, and (4) the *komissi* to inspect the stores and restaurants. When meetings are held, only the election of the two inspection committees seems to have any real significance. The director, the dues, and the store allotments are all decided further up the cooperative and governmental hierarchy. Actually, very little autonomy is possessed by the basic units (Gogol', 1957, p. 106).*

There is one more important difference that must be noted. The goal of Western cooperative stores is to provide lower prices for its members. In the Soviet Union, on the other hand, not only are yearly rebates frequently the exception but the rule is that rural consumers' goods prices are 7 per cent higher than equivalent urban rates. Government stores generally have lower prices than cooperative stores (Kondrashev, 1956, p. 172; Kondrashev, *Dengy i Kredit*, No. 9, 1958, p. 22; Gogol', 1958, p. 261). While this is partially due to additional transportation costs, in effect it is an additional tax burden the peasant must bear. Furthermore, consumer cooperative prices are set by Ministry of Trade officials, often in conjunction with the Council of Ministers, not by the management of the cooperative stores.

Consequently, one must be wary of attempts to link Rochdale cooperatives and Soviet consumer cooperatives.† If anything, the general organization of Russian consumer cooperatives is similar to that of the Soviet government store network. A hierarchy arises from the local outlet until the peak is reached at the republic and all-Union

---

* This reference contains complaints about the lack of participation in consumer cooperatives and plans for improvement in the future.

† Even the payment of dividends is not the same as in the West. Thus, when dividends are paid to shareholders, the payment is based on the store profits, not on individual patronage as is the main pattern elsewhere (*Report of the American Marketing Delegation to the Soviet Union*, 1960, p. 11).

levels. Not only are the operational patterns similar but many of the control and planning functions of both organizations are exercised through the same offices. (See Figure 3.)

The bureaucratic staff of the consumer cooperative stores is usually smaller than its counterpart in the government store because of the smaller size of the cooperative outlets. None the less, as one moves up the administrative network, the bureaucracy grows just as rapidly. The village cooperative societies (*sel'po*) are joined together in regional unions (*raipotrebsoiuz*). They operate the larger regional stores and supervise the operation of the societies and supply them with goods. Commission trade operations —which will be discussed shortly—are also their responsibility. Theoretically the regional union is made up of society representatives and reflects their feelings, although in practice it is inevitably the reverse. The regional unions (*raipotrebsoiuzy*) and the various subregional unions (*raipo*) are joined together to form state (*oblast*), county (*krai*), or autonomous republic union; these in turn are linked together to form a republic union, which is then joined into an all-Union consumer cooperative (*Tsentralsoiuz*). Each level is supposedly composed of delegations from the lower levels; however, as was true in the regional unions, the orders come from the top down. The senior levels administer the lower levels, carry on the wholesaling function, and handle sales of surplus agricultural products and raw materials procured by the regional union and the society.

The structure of the all-Union Cooperative Society (*Tsentralsoiuz*) as of September 14, 1957, was as follows: (1) the Congress (*S'ezd*) of Delegates of the consumer cooperatives of the USSR, which meets once every four

Figure 3—The Structure of the Consumer Cooperative Organization

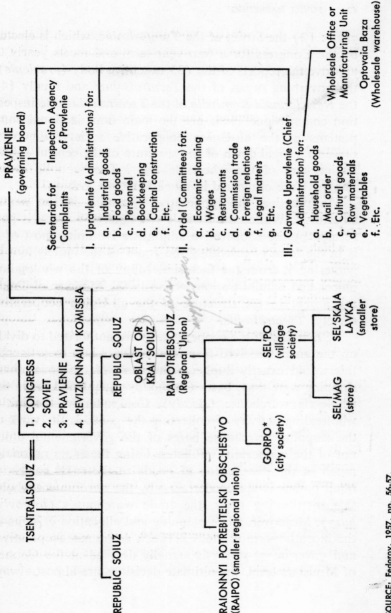

TSENTRALSOIUZ
1. CONGRESS
2. SOVIET
3. PRAVLENIE
4. REVIZIONNAIA KOMISSIA

PRAVLENIE (governing board)

Secretariat for Complaints

Inspection Agency of Pravlenie

I. Upravlenie (Administrations) for:
a. Industrial goods
b. Food goods
c. Personnel
d. Bookkeeping
e. Capital construction
f. Etc.

II. Otdel (Committees) for:
a. Economic planning
b. Wages
c. Commission trade
d. Restaurants
e. Foreign relations
f. Legal matters
g. Etc.

III. Glavnoe Upravlenie (Chief Administration) for:
a. Household goods
b. Mail order
c. Cultural goods
d. Raw materials
e. Vegetables
f. Etc.

Wholesale Office or Manufacturing Unit
Optovaia Baza (Wholesale warehouse)

REPUBLIC SOIUZ

REPUBLIC SOIUZ

OBLAST OR KRAI SOIUZ

RAIPOTREBSOIUZ (Regional Union)

RAIONNYI POTREBITELSKI OBSCHESTVO (RAIPO) (smaller regional union)

GORPO* (city society)

SEL'PO (village society)

SEL'MAG (store)

SEL'SKAIA LAVKA (smaller store)

SOURCE: Fedorov, 1957, pp. 56-57.

* Responsible for Commission Trade and the limited number of consumer cooperatives found in the city.

years: (2) the Soviet of the *Tsentralsoiuz,* which is elected
by the Congress for a four-year term and meets yearly to
approve the reports of the (3) executive body (*pravlenie*),
the governing organ of the *Tsentralsoiuz;* and finally (4)
the *Revizionnaia Komissiia* of the *Tsentralsoiuz,* the inspection commission. These are the main organizational components of the all-Union cooperative society. Figure 3
presents a breakdown of the structure of the central organization and of the wholesale units. The republic *soiuzi*
(unions) are organized in much the same fashion.

In practice, the cooperative system is not so neatly
structured. While considerable wholesaling activity is performed by the cooperative administrative units, most of it
is in the form of providing the goods to the outlets, not in
gathering it from the factories. Many of the wholesaling
offices and administrations active in the Ministry of Trade
are absent in the structure of the all-Union cooperative
society, *Tsentralsoiuz.*

Obviously, if the cooperatives were authorized to divide
up the goods received from the factories into assortments,
this would exactly duplicate the work of the government
shipping warehouse bases (*vykhodnye bazy*) and the initial
wholesale warehouse (*sklady*). Consequently, the initial
wholesaling activity of collecting the goods is the work of
the shipping warehouse bases of the governmental units,
not of the cooperative affiliates. Using the same rationale,
much of the distribution of goods to the rural consumer
retail outlets is also undertaken by the government wholesale distributing units, the trade warehouses (*torgovlye
bazy*). Moreover, while planning and allocation of some of
the more important goods between consumer cooperatives
and government stores is actually decided at the Council
of Ministers level, the ultimate decisions are almost always

based on the advice of the Minister of Trade or are completely delegated to the Ministry of Trade and its wholesaling subsidiary (Vasil'ev, *et al.*, 1958, Vol. II, pp. 18–21, 26–27; Genkin and Fialkov, 1957, p. 20; Fedorov, 1957, pp. 10, 55; *Sovetskaia Torgovlia*, Jan. 4, 1958, p. 3). Thus, the authority of the *Tsentralsoiuz* system is sharply limited, even when dealing with such basic questions as price, volume, and allocation of commodities. This seems to be further evidence that the Soviet cooperative system lacks autonomy comparable to that possessed by Western cooperatives.

Table 3—Cooperative Sales, Rural, Urban, Tsentralsoiuz (in Billions of Rubles)

Year	Retail Turnover of Rural (1) and Cooperative (2) Trade Network Including Restaurants		Retail Turnover of Tsentralsoiuz	Cooperative Trade Minus Rural (2—1)	Tsentralsoiuz Trade Minus Rural (3—1)
	(1)	(2)	(3)	(4)	(5)
1940	5.164	4.700	4.217	—0.464	—0.947
1945	4.178	3.554	3.433	—0.614	—0.735
1946	5.609	4.870	4.679	—0.739	—0.930
1947	5.878	7.906	7.042	2.208	1.164
1948	6.350	7.775	7.067	1.425	0.717
1949	7.544	9.225	8.436	1.681	0.892
1950	8.660	9.854	9.051	1.194	0.391
1951	9.455	10.584	9.649	1.129	0.194
1952	9.766	10.870	9.927	1.104	0.161
1953	10.780	12.203	11.150	1.432	0.370
1954	12.608	14.623	13.534	2.015	0.926
1955	13.327	15.458	14.480	2.131	1.153
1956	14.585	16.681	16.135	2.096	1.550
1957	16.436	19.205	18.917	2.769	2.481
1958	17.421	20.926	20.581	3.505	3.160
1959	17.802	22.116	21.728	4.314	3.926
1960	18.880	23.651	23.651	4.771	4.771

SOURCE: TsSU 5, pp. 681, 684.

There are some special features about cooperative trade that must be fitted in if the description of domestic marketing is to be complete. As Table 3 shows, the official figure for cooperative sales exceeded the total rural sales. The difference amounted to 4.771 billion rubles in 1960. The explanation of the excess of cooperative sales over rural sales is accounted for by the activities of producer cooperatives and commission trade as well as the decision to allow the reappearance of consumer cooperatives in the city.

Producer cooperative sales until 1960 were generally included within the broad classification of cooperative sales even though the former is not a part of the consumer cooperative network. Located in the cities, producer cooperatives were usually composed of individual artisans who made handicraft or household goods and who found it more expedient to unite together than to work separately. In the past, such groups have played an important role in Soviet society, since they were one of the few organizations that made repairs and provided services for the Russian household. Producer cooperatives have had their own hierarchy reaching into the all-Union level. In 1955, producer cooperative sales amounted to almost 1 billion rubles. (See Table 3, column 2 minus column 3.) In 1956, the Russians reclassified the bulk of the producer cooperative activities into their regular industrial statistics. As a result, official producer cooperative sales immediately declined and, by 1958 and 1959, had fallen to 350 million rubles. Today they no longer exist as a special category of distribution activity, but until 1960 sales of producer cooperatives accounted for a portion of the cooperative sales made in urban areas.

With the aim of offsetting the role of the *kolkhoz* markets, consumer cooperative societies were authorized in 1953 to introduce commission trade into the Soviet marketing system (Goldman, 1958, p. 136). Under the control of *Otdely Gorodskoi Kooperativnoi Torgovli* (Committees of Urban Cooperative Trade), consumer cooperatives were encouraged to accept agricultural commodities on a commission basis from either the *kolkhoz* or the *kolkhoznik*. They would then sell the goods in commission trade stores that were to be opened in the *kolkhoz* markets or in shops of consumer cooperative trade organizations. For this the consumer cooperatives collect a commission fee of approximately 10 per cent of the price received by the producer.* Upon delivery, the producer receives a share of the estimated sales price in advance. As of January, 1961, the down payment was increased from 50 to 75 per cent. The remainder is paid upon completion of the sale. The *kolkhoz* or *kolkhoznik* retains the title and bears the risk in the meantime.

As one might suspect, such a system has been subject to considerable abuse, and there have been many calls for reforms. None the less, despite serious shortcomings, commission trade permits an increased division of labor and allows the peasant to market his surplus without having to leave his fields.

As can be seen from Table 1, commission trade grew rapidly in its early years. By March, 1961, there were 15,000 outlets selling food on commission (*Sovetskaia Torgovlia*, March 16, 1961, p. 1). The majority of these outlets were located in urban areas, with the result that approximately 65 per cent of the commission sales were

---

* The figure of 10 per cent was obtained by comparing the amount received by *kolkhozy* and *kolkhozniky* with the total amount of commission sales (TsSU 3, p. 787).

transacted there. (See Table 4.) This proportion accounts for an additional 570 million rubles of cooperative sales that were made in urban areas.

**Table 4—Commission Trade in Cities and Villages for 1957
(in Billions of Rubles)**

Retail turnover in cities and suburbs including commission trade	46.060
Retail turnover in cities and suburbs excluding commission trade	45.490
Commission trade in cities and suburbs	0.570
Retail turnover in villages including commission trade	16.440
Retail turnover in villages excluding commission trade	16.240
Commission trade in villages	0.200

SOURCE: Data derived from *Vestnik Statistiki,* No. 8, 1958, p. 81.

Therefore, out of the total consumer cooperative sales in urban areas shown in column 4 of Table 3, almost 1.9 billion rubles in 1957 (2.769 billion rubles less 288 million rubles of producer cooperative sales and 570 million rubles arising from commission trade) and 4 billion rubles in 1960 (4.771 billion rubles minus 700 million rubles) is unaccounted for. This indicates the sales volume of cooperative stores located in smaller or more remote cities. On occasion, cooperative stores simply take the place of the government store network if the consumer cooperative channels of communication are already established. Moreover, in March, 1959, the government announced that it would again permit the opening of consumer cooperatives in some cities and suburbs (*Sovetskaia Torgovlia,* March 12 and 24, 1959, p. 1). Yet on the whole, it still seems accurate to say that consumer cooperative trade is confined to rural areas and that government stores are excluded from the consumer cooperative monopoly in these areas. The main exception to this jurisdictional division is the network of *kolkhoz,* or collective farm markets, which overlaps into both areas. It is this phenomenon that will be described now.

(Collective Farm) THE KOLKHOZ MARKETS (Free)

Despite urbanization and suburbanization, farmers' markets (Haymarket Square in Boston, Les Halles in Paris) continue to thrive in many European and American cities. Consequently, the appearance of the same phenomenon in the Soviet Union should not come as a surprise. What does strike one is the much more important role such institutions, known as *kolkhoz* (collective farm) markets, play in Russia. While their portion of total retail sales (as shown in Table 5) is relatively minor compared to what it once was, their share in total food sales, which is almost the only thing sold on such markets, is more significant. As seen in Table 6, their share of total food sales volume was 20 per cent in 1940 and as high as 51 per cent in 1945 (an abnormal war year), although it too has fallen in recent years.*

---

* When citing the sales volume of *kolkhoz* markets, apparently only urban sales are included. If rural *kolkhoz* market sales are included, the share of *kolkhoz* market sales to total retail sales would have been approximately 19 per cent in 1940 instead of the usually cited figure of 14.3 per cent as given in Table 5. This is based on Lifits (1950), p. 236. An indication of total urban and rural *kolkhoz* market sales in 1952 is given in "Ustranit' Nedostatki v Organizatsii Kolkhoznoi Torgovli," *Sovetskaia Torgovlia* (Feb., 1954), p. 3. As opposed to the official figure of 12.9 per cent (TsSU 6, p. 19) for urban *kolkhoz* market sales, a figure of 14.4 per cent for all *kolkhoz* market sales is cited. This would mean sales were 6.62 billion rubles instead of 5.37 billion rubles, Table 1.

Table 5—The Share of Total Retail Sales by the Three Main Trade Networks in the Soviet Union
(in Percentages) *

	1932	1940	1945	1950	1955	1956	1957	1958	1959	1960
Government stores	30	62.7	42	63.9	63.2	64.6	65.1	65.2	65.7	66.8
Cooperative stores	53	23.0	12	24.1	28.1	28.3	28.9	29.2	29.2	28.8
Urban kolkhoz markets	17	14.3	46	12.0	8.7	7.1	6.0	5.6	5.1	4.4

Table 6—The Share of All Food Sales by the Three Main Trade Networks in the Soviet Union
(in Percentages)*

	1932	1940	1945	1950	1955	1956	1957	1958	1959	1960
Government stores	26	61.5	38	63.3	63.8	65	66	90.6	91.7	92.6
Cooperative stores	48	18.3	11	18.6	21.5	23	24			
Urban kolkhoz markets	26	20.2	51	18.1	14.7	12	10	9.4	8.3	7.4

Table 7—The Share of Retail Sales of Food Items Sold Jointly by Each of Three Main Trade Networks (in Percentages) *

	1932	1940	1945	1950	1955	1956	1957	1958	1959	1960
Government and Cooperative Stores		69.8		71.3	74.6	78.9	81.8	82.7	84.6	86.2
Urban kolkhoz markets		30.2		28.7	25.4	21.1	18.2	17.3	15.4	13.8

SOURCE: TsSU 3, p. 707; TsSU 5, p. 680; TsSU 6, p. 19; TsSU 8, p. 427.

*TsSU 2 (pp. 228-29) gives a different set of figures showing that the portion of the kolkhoz markets was higher. The data apparently have been reclassified, since TsSU 6 shows the same figures as TsSU 2.

A clearer picture of the role of the *kolkhoz* market is obtained by considering some of its other characteristics. In certain areas, *kolkhoz* market sales are very important. In a city like Odessa, *kolkhoz* markets accounted for 60 per cent of the food sales in 1955 and 42 per cent of the food sales in 1956. However, a more crucial factor to be taken into account is the share of sales of only those varieties of foods actually sold on the *kolkhoz* markets in comparison with the sales of these same goods in government and cooperative trade. Since the *kolkhoz* markets are primarily outlets for the surplus produce of the *kolkhoz* farms and the *kolkhozniky,* this excludes the sale of canned goods and most processed foods, and includes mainly fresh vegetables, grain and livestock products, meat and milk. In the sale of the goods that are not excluded the role of the *kolkhoz* market is greater and accounted for as much as 31 per cent of such sales in 1940, although it had fallen to 14 per cent in 1960. (See Table 7.)

There are a considerable number of *kolkhoz* markets. In the larger cities they abound near railroad stations and other points of natural population flow. Moscow has at least thirty, and Odessa eight. *Kolkhoz* markets are divided about equally between rural and urban areas, although the largest and best are located in the cities where they have the greatest sales volume. Although their growth has slackened in the last few years, as of December, 1961, there were over 9,000 *kolkhoz* markets throughout the country. Absolute volume of sales on the *kolkhoz* markets has also dropped since 1950.

The Russians refer to the *kolkhoz* market as a free market (or unorganized), thereby maintaining that within limits prices are determined by the interaction of the free

forces of supply and demand (Serebriakov, 1956, p. 70).*
Generally, prices in the *kolkhoz* markets are above those
in the government stores. This is contrary to Western experience, where prices in farmers' markets are usually below those of supermarkets and groceries. In the past this
has been largely the result of poor pricing policy in the
Russian government stores, where prices have been set too
low relative to the inadequate supplies. However, part of
the price difference is, in a sense, a premium paid for the
better quality and freshness of the *kolkhoz* market products, an indication of unsatisfactory service in government
stores.

The *kolkhoz* markets are administered by a branch of
the local city trade organization. In addition to seeing that
the market runs smoothly, this branch is responsible for
attracting the outlying collective farms to its particular
market, signing contracts, and providing transportation and
stalls for the goods of both the *kolkhozniky* and *kolkhozy*.
Advertisements are periodically placed in the local press
to attract both supplies and customers. The market administrators are also to provide sanitary marketing facilities
as well as living accommodations for its users. Finally, the
administration levies a daily franchise tax on all sellers who
desire to use the market facilities.

---

* Basile Kerblay, a French economist, considers that the indirect
control by the state is considerable.

CONCLUSION

An attempt has been made to present the main features of the distribution system in the Soviet Union. Attention has been devoted to the structure of both the government store and the consumer cooperative network. The types of outlets available, as well as the respective chains of command, have been described.

Some similarities between the basic trade functions performed by trade organizations in the state-controlled Soviet system and those in the atomistically operated system of the West were noted. Although there are more variations and elaborations in the West, both systems have a basic three-way division of functions into retailing, wholesaling, and manufacturing. However, there appears to be greater centralization and administrative control in the Soviet Union, especially at the wholesale level. Furthermore, all marketing activity is an extension of government activity. This would seem to be the major difference between the two systems.

Within the Soviet Union, there is considerable similarity between the government and consumer cooperative trade networks. In fact, there seems to be more similarity between the Soviet government store network and the Soviet consumer cooperative network than between the foreign consumer cooperatives and the Soviet version. Because of the many interactions at the various administrative levels, there is some question as to whether or not the consumer cooperatives have any significant independence from the Ministry of Trade and its government store network.

Although the development of commission sales and the limited movement of the consumer cooperatives into the cities suggests a slight change in policy, there appears to be little competition between the major Soviet trade networks. The main competitive force apparently comes from the *kolkhoz* markets. They compete directly with food stores of the government in the city and the cooperative network in the country. In turn, a desire by the state to compete with the *kolkhoz* market apparently was a major factor for the introduction and growth of commission trade.

The purpose of this chapter has been the modest one of outlining the basic structure of domestic trade in the Soviet Union. Despite the organizational changes of the last few years, there has been little basic change in the marketing functions performed by the government. Having laid the groundwork in these initial pages, it now becomes possible to discuss some of the operating techniques and problems. It is to this aspect of the topic that we turn in Chapter 3.

[3] *PLANNING THE DISTRIBUTION OF CONSUMER GOODS*

INTRODUCTION

*I*THE ACTUAL ESTABLISHMENT of goals and norms in the early five-year plans, the newer seven-year plan, the yearly aggregate plans, and the planned quotas for individual factories and enterprises is perhaps the Soviet's greatest contribution to economic theory and development. No one would argue that every industrial goal has been attained precisely or that every facet of industrial production is measurable in terms of goals. Still, with some important exceptions, the Soviet Union for some years has consistently met and/or surpassed its targets in the top priority area of heavy industry. Although overfulfillment itself may be an indication that total planning is not as balanced and coordinated as the Russians would have one believe, the fact that a formerly backward country is now the world's second industrial power indicates that the Soviet system of industrial planning has had some degree of success.

While planning has made its greatest impact in the sphere of heavy industrial production, the directors of the Soviet economy have also extended their planning techniques to the field of trade and distribution.

The law of balanced proportionate development of the national economy that operates in our society calls for the conscious and organized coordination of production and consumption. Since our economy is planned, we can directly and not in a round-about way calculate demand and develop production accordingly. Herein lie the tremendous advantages of our system (Mikoyan, 1954, p. 19).

The following pages explore the special problems connected with planning the distribution of consumers' goods. In order to concentrate on the tasks confronting marketing officials, it will be assumed that the basic decisions concerning the relative role of consumers' goods in the national economy have already been made. Such questions as the division of capital funds and national resources between heavy industry, consumers' goods production, exports and stockpiles will not concern us. These are matters to be determined by higher political authorities. Within this context, there remain the tasks of first, dividing up the resources between various consumers' goods industries and, second, allocating the produced consumers' goods to the various retail outlets throughout the country. The goods must be distributed so that the consumers will be able to buy them. This involves estimating consumer demands and then supplying them with the proper goods. Procedures for the estimation of demand and the allocation of goods, as officially set forth, will be considered and subsequently contrasted with the various problems that have arisen in the actual performance of these tasks.

FORMULATION OF THE PLAN

Demand Estimation

The procedure for calculating demand is outlined in numerous Soviet sources (Serebriakov, 1956, p. 150; Khrekin, 1957, p. 10, 1958, p. 47; Abutkova, 1954; Itin, 1951; Rostovskii-Na Donu, 1957, p. 232). Although there is some disagreement, most Russian authorities say that the process should begin with an estimate of the over-all purchasing power of the population. While this may appear to be a difficult task, actually it would not be hard to do in the Soviet Union. Since the state controls all but an infinitesimal part of the economy, the statistical sources are readily available. All the planner has to do is to subtract population expenditures for taxes, services, contributions, and savings from income that consists of wages and salaries, earnings of *kolkhozniky,* pensions, student stipends, and miscellaneous income. The answer, which will approximate 75 per cent of total personal income, represents the purchasing fund or disposable income of the population.

Several organizations normally have to cooperate to provide such information. The all-Union Gosplan, the state planning organization, is the main coordinating office. Since much of their work was decentralized after 1957, the republic offices of Gosplan have assumed more responsibility. The regional economic councils (*sovnarkhozy*) have also taken a more active role. In addition, Gosplan works closely throughout with the various central and regional offices of the Ministry of Trade. The Central Statistical

Administration (TsSU), Gosbank (the state bank) and *Tsentralsoiuz* (consumer cooperative) also participate in the preparation of the estimates.

Given the over-all figure for disposable income, the next step is to break it down into smaller geographical subdivisions. Officially this is supposed to continue until data are obtained for *oblasts,* for cities, and in some cases for specific neighborhoods.

Equipped with the figure of disposable income, the planners are then presumably able to estimate what the ruble sales volume of consumers' goods will be. However, before they can determine how much will be spent in the government and cooperative networks, they must deduct the predicted sales of *kolkhoz* markets. On the assumption that such information is available, it is then possible to estimate over-all per capita expenditures in state-controlled outlets.

The next step in the planning process is to predict the consumption of specific classes of goods and to break down the assortment of each commodity. The planner must ascertain for each region, for example, how many apples will be consumed compared with the number of oranges and how many consumers will prefer white bread to black bread. To obtain this information, the government has access to individual budget studies. The Central Statistical Administration regularly conducts such studies among a selected sample of 40,000 workers, white-collar employees, and *kolkhozniki.* For instance, the Central Statistical Administration of Belorussia systematically surveys the budgets of 300 working families. Leningrad uses the family budgets of 839 workers and 346 white-collar employees. In Moscow and Kiev, the budgets of 1,057 workers and 506 white-collar families are covered (*Report of the*

American Marketing Delegation to the Soviet Union, 1960, p. 18; TsSU12, 1958, p. 143; Statisticheskoe Upravlenie, Goroda Leningrada, 1957, p. 68; Shkrebel', No. 1, 1957, p. 67).

Although the precise sampling techniques do not seem to have been explicitly discussed by the Russians, many writers have outlined the basic criteria. Generally it is necessary to consider "the population's social characteristics, their professions, and their nationalities." The region's cultural and living standards and the climatic conditions also have an effect on the volume, structure, and character of consumption and therefore must be reflected in the sample (Serebriakov, 1956, p. 151; Trakhtenberg and Sablina, 1957, p. 9).

By means of such budget studies, the trade organization is then in a position to compile data on per capita consumption of such items as bread and sugar. While a given individual may not like bread, an over-all pattern of bread consumption for a specific locality can be derived. A similar procedure will permit the planners to estimate sales of other consumers' products as well as expected sales in a given geographical area.

Once this information is made available to the trade administration in the area, the estimates are supposedly substantiated through investigations undertaken by the various stores themselves. Although in placing their orders some organizations are reported to have used per capita data literally, the store management is supposed to supplement the per capita data with sales trends, seasonal requirements, inventory turnover, and the consultation and advice of sales personnel in the store. In addition, stores and trade organizations are encouraged to organize direct conferences with consumers to hear their suggestions. With this purpose in mind, special stores for new goods, *novinok,* have been opened to test consumer reaction to new products. Displays and fashion shows in stores and clubs, as well as *Dom Modelei* (style centers) further attempt to sound out the consumer.

Several stores have also experimented with more elaborate statistical interviewing techniques (Nemchinov, 1955, Vol. 1, p. 257; Hunter, 1960, p. 26). A less complicated and more commonplace approach is to place complaint and suggestion books and forms throughout the store. This writer can testify from personal experience that they are used. As a result of such analysis, the store has at its disposal data regarding quantity, quality, assortment, and seasonal fluctuations.

Finally, local demand is affected by planning moves such as the construction of a new recreation center or a television station. Since these decisions are all made by the government, it has the power to expand trade facilities and stocks accordingly. Consequently, the state is not only in a position to plan for an increase in the sales volume of a given area; but, through the establishment of sales norms per salesclerk, it can also anticipate the need for increased counter space and plan the locational pattern by adding retail and wholesale outlets.

Processing of the Demand Estimates

Relying on the information that has been gathered, marketing officials are then able to place specific orders for goods that eventually will take the form of inventory on the shelves. The provision of goods is brought about by measures taken at the top and bottom of the chain of command. It is a circular procedure. On the one hand, allocation plans are made at upper echelons and handed down through channels. On the other hand, specific requests and orders (*zaiavki* and *zakazy*) of stores and trade organizations are sent upward asking for a quota of goods or seeking shipment of an already authorized quota. In turn, the higher authorities use the submitted requests and orders to help draw up their allocation plans.

The goods the state considers to be most important are centrally allocated. They are placed in a *rynochnyi fond,* which literally means that the goods are part of a state fund. A system of priorities is established, and the output is allocated according to the existing priority system. Given the production of a particular type of goods, demands and supplies are matched by constructing material balances in much the same way that goods are allocated in heavy industry (Levine, 1959, p. 151; Montias, Dec., 1959, p. 962). If demand should exceed supply, those whose needs are considered to be most important are accorded a higher priority and receive delivery.

Planning the distribution of consumers' goods is less complex than planning in heavy industry, however, since there is less interdependence in the decisions that are made about consumers' goods. For example, in heavy industry, the order to reallocate a fixed amount of coal to steel mills instead of to railroad locomotives may necessitate a change in the transportation and production scheduling plans of many industries, including an additional change in the steel industry. However, since consumers' goods are generally not used as components in the production of other goods, such feedback or readjustment of all material balances is usually not necessary in the allocation of consumers' goods. If wants are greater than the supply, the frequent solution is to send the available goods where the need is most critical.

Other outlets are asked to accommodate themselves to the supplies already on hand and theoretically the matter is ended.*

Prior to the reorganization of the latter 1950's, the allocation plans for those consumers' goods that were centrally allocated were drawn up by the Ministry of Trade of the USSR or the Council of Ministers of the USSR with the help of Gosplan. With the abolition of the Ministry of Trade of the USSR, this function was transferred to Gosplan, the Republican Ministries of Trade, and the regional and republic economic councils (*sovnarkhozy*).

As a result of the most recent change, some items are centrally allocated not only by republic and trade sectors (that is, government or cooperative networks) but by state (*oblast*) and by city. The number of products so classified varies according to the existing stage of the organizational cycle. If the vogue is centralization, as it was prior to 1957, then more goods are included. If the fashion is decentralization, then fewer items are subject to such centralized regulation. During the 1958 era of decentralization, the *rynochnyi fond* consisted of thirty-eight items as opposed to 150 consumers' goods in the years before 1957. This included the following: flour, groats, sugar, cotton and wool fabrics, sewn products, and leather and felt shoes.† These goods represented a minimum of controlled commodities. In times of increased control, other items are added to this core.

---

* It may not be this simple in all instances. It may be necessary to make price adjustments in order to prevent disruptions in the distribution process. (See Chapter 4.)

† Information obtained from A. I. Smirnov, Director of Soiuzglavtorg (Goldman, 1959, p. 38). Bespalov says that forty-two items are in the *rynochnyi fond,* thirty-five of which are controlled by Gosplan and seven by Republic authorities (Vasil'ev, *et al.,* 1958, p. 17).

Other categories of consumers' goods are subject to somewhat less control. A class previously called "regulated commodities" is next in importance. These items do not have as high a priority and are not considered to be in critical supply; therefore, control over them is less detailed and less centralized. Formerly the Ministry of Trade of both the USSR and the republics had planning and allocative responsibility for these goods with no recourse to the Council of Ministers or Gosplan. Now planning is carried out by Soiuzglavtorg and Gosplan, which have assumed some of the functions of the Ministry of Trade of the USSR and the republic ministries of trade. At present there are about 400 such goods. Included are such items as coffee, tea, jam, dishware, household goods, and soaps, which are in short supply in some republics and more abundant in others. Finally, for those goods produced locally or not covered by priorities, the only allocative arrangement used is a system of local and direct contractual agreements between the parties concerned.

Within such a framework of relative priorities, the various trade organizations order their goods. At the store level, the buyer (*tovaroved*) is responsible for maintaining the goods assortment that his department carries. The needs of the various buyers are compiled and approved by the manager's administrative staff, which then submits requests and orders (*zaiavki* and *zakazy*) for goods. Although the buyers may have considerable discretion, frequently they are authorized to do no more than request delivery of goods that have already been allocated under the plan of retail sales as prepared by the upper echelons. The existing plan, in turn, may have been based on the requests and orders of previous periods.

At this stage, the flow chart varies depending on the

nature of the goods ordered and the importance of the store submitting the order. If the store is large and important or if the goods are locally produced and not subject to centralized control, the order may be submitted directly to the producer. Typically, however, the requests and orders are forwarded, along with similar requests from other stores, to the trade department of the local city trade organization (*torg*). If the item is available and the enterprise is authorized by the previously prepared plan to order it, the buyer for the trade organization (*torg tovaroved*) instructs the *torg* warehouse to deliver the goods to the store.

To replenish its stocks, the *torg* in turn submits its order to the next highest trade organization at the state or county (*oblast* or *krai*) level. Again, whether or not the orders are transmitted further along the chain of command or are handled at this stage is dependent on the importance of the *torg,* its geographical location, and the nature of the goods. Unless the goods are procured from local producers, the requests and orders are sent from the local trade organization to the wholesale office (*kontor*) or administration (*upravlenie*), which processes them and requests its wholesale trading warehouses (*torgovlyi bazy*) to send the goods to the requesting retail warehouse. As seen in Figure 4, the requisitions and order forms are passed to the initial wholesale structure (*vykhodnaia baza*) which is also administered by an office or administration. In a sense, it is here that the whole distribution procedure begins, since the sales (*torgovo-sbyt*) organization of the industrial ministry releases its output to the consumer market by complying with requests and orders sent to the factory by the shipping warehouse.

Orders from wholesale units to factories are sent in a variety of ways. They may emanate from the superior

Figure 4—The Wholesaling Procedure in the Soviet Union

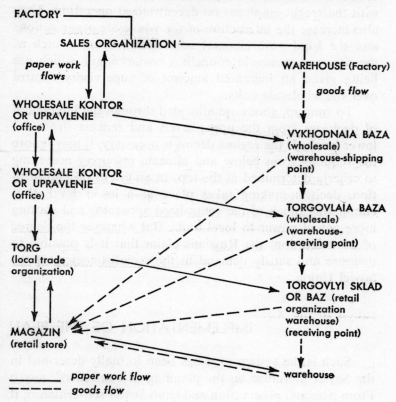

wholesale organization and funnel through the industrial ministries, which since 1957 have been operating at the republic level. As has been mentioned before, it is entirely possible, however, to short-circuit many of the intermediary agencies. For example, more and more orders are being issued by the office or administration of the warehouse, and sometimes by the *torg* itself, directly to the sales organization of the factory. Such transactions better accord with the recent emphasis on decentralized operation. They also increase the interaction of the wholesale organizations and the local governmental administrative units, such as the regional economic councils (*sovnarkhozy*) which are being given an increased amount of supervisory control over the wholesale units.

To sum up, goods are allocated through the interaction of decisions from the upper levels and requests from the lower levels. If the regime deems it necessary, it may ignore the requests from below and allocate resources according to criteria determined at the top. In an era of decentralization, decision-making takes place at a lower level, thus eliminating much of the centralized apparatus and shifting more actual power to local units. But whatever the degree of centralization, the Russians claim that it is possible to measure and satisfy demand in the socialist society of the Soviet Union.

IMPLEMENTATION OF THE PLAN

Such is the system as it has been formally described in the Soviet literature on the planning of consumers' goods. From personal observation and from Soviet self-criticism, it seems that planning the distribution of Russian consumers' goods has not always been as elaborate or precise as some of its more outspoken proponents assert. There are at least three reasons for this: (1) planning inflexibilities that arise because of production below anticipated levels and scarcity of resources, (2) misallocation of commodities due to human miscalculation, and (3) the unpredictability of the consumer once certain basic needs have been satisfied.

The Effect of Unfulfilled Production Targets
and Scarcity of Resources

While a discussion of production problems is outside the scope of this study, it is impossible to ignore certain consequences of the Russian production process when analyzing marketing in the Soviet Union. For example, if the supplies promised to marketing officials are not produced, it becomes all but impossible to implement the allocation plans fully. Unfortunately, a consistent feature of domestic trade in the Soviet Union has been that production goals for consumers' goods have not been met. There are several reasons for this.

One of the more important is that agricultural output has been difficult to predict. Not only has food production fallen far short of its goals; but until recently there was no significant growth over the preplanning output levels of 1926–1927. While there are major political, sociological, and cultural reasons for this, there is also the unpredictable effect of nature. No matter how carefully one plans or how much priority one attaches to plan fulfillment of a given crop, if the rainfall is too much or too little or the weather too hot or too cold, production suffers. Since food constitutes more than 50 per cent of all retail trade volume, it seems clear that fluctuations in agricultural production inevitably make it difficult to plan prospective trade stocks. The fact that agricultural raw materials, such as wool, cotton, and leather, are important in many consumers' goods other than food further affects the availability of supplies for trade and distribution.

Another obstacle to planning the allocation of consumption stocks is the fact that the production of Soviet consumers' goods has always been expendable. Any shortcomings of output in other important economic sectors almost invariably are felt in light industry and consumption. The available resources are always allocated first to the high-priority sectors of heavy industry and only then do they spill over to the nonessential areas of trade. As a result, many of the initially planned goals for consumers' goods or light industrial production in the five-year plans have subsequently been reduced or simply underfulfilled. Continual revision of production expectations and the consequent uncertainty as to the size of the stocks available for distribution would seem to suggest that the official version of the allocation procedure is only a superficial description.

There is another false bottom in the ideal planning framework. Whether based on an *oblast,* republic, or all-Union plan, the details must all be drawn up months in advance. Those familiar with budget preparation procedures for governmental organizations in the United States are well aware of the complications. This applies whether the budget estimates are sought in small army units or large Washington bureaus. Requests for July, 1963, are required as early as Fall, 1961. Those who find that the estimates carefully compiled in 1961 for needs (not to mention organizations) that no longer exist in 1963 can well appreciate the inflexibility of long-range planning.

Timing is also a problem in the Soviet Union. Of necessity, plans must be drawn up at least a year in advance in over-all monetary and physical units. Forty-five days before the actual delivery period, more detailed requests are reportedly made as to sizes, colors, style, and quality of fabrics. Despite the possibility of making short-run adjustments, the difficulties connected with drawing up a plan in time frequently mean that an enterprise simply operates without an officially approved plan. (*Sovetskaia Torgovlia,* Jan. 5, 1960, p. 1). Moreover, it has also been reported that when changes are made they are often made without the consent of the recipient (*Sovetskaia Torgovlia,* Aug. 30, 1960, p. 2).

Once the plan is set, the very nature of a system propelled by goal fulfillment results in further inflexibility. The Russians themselves acknowledge this built-in rigidity. One writer complained that once a production quota is set, the factory and its employees, who receive premiums for fulfillment of the given quota, refuse to readjust the production mix to allow for shifts in demand (Mochalov, No. 8, 1958, p. 57; *Pravda,* Jan. 5, 1960, p. 5). He further complained that if the goals are set in general value terms, instead of in precise qualitative and quantitative terms, the factory may end up producing silk dresses when the consumers' demand may be for cotton dresses. Since it takes fewer silk dresses to meet a quota in gross value terms, it is easier for the factory to fulfill the plan if silk, rather than cotton, dresses are produced. Because the interests of the factory manager and his employees are dictated by the production plan, and since the production goals do not always coincide with the desires of the consumers, the consumers are likely to be the ones who suffer.

Naturally, if the planners are unable to rely on a pre-planned flow of goods from the production and supply sectors, it becomes very difficult to ascertain consumers' demands. If production and supply are disrupted, unsatisfied consumers temporarily switch to other substitutes. As a result, it becomes hard to determine what consumers would have purchased if the missing goods had been available. In 1956 it was estimated that demand for manufactured consumers' goods was underfulfilled by an amount equal to approximately 5 per cent of the total retail sales volume (Rostovskii na Donu, 1957, p. 242). But since the consumers were not satisfied, how is it possible to calculate what specific types and quantities of goods would have been purchased? Gogol' sees yet another aspect of the problem. If production of consumers' goods is inadequate, even that which is sold is an inaccurate picture of what demand actually is and will be in the future. Scare-buying and hoarding inevitably distort the normal sales flow and make the planners' job all the more difficult (Goldman, 1959, p. 27).

Under such conditions, whatever is produced is likely to be sold. Regardless of the fact that the quality may be poor, the size may not fit, and the color may be faded, the consumer must often buy since there is no other alternative. If one trade organization rejects the goods because of their poor quality, another immediately accepts them. Furthermore, there is no guarantee that the first trade organization will receive high-quality goods in the future. Clearly, estimation of consumers' demands under such conditions cannot be gauged accurately.

Given the existing priority scale, an attempt to implement a locational plan will be handicapped also. As long as building resources for distribution outlets are subordinated to the more urgent needs of heavy industrial and housing construction, the attempt by marketing officials to construct a planned locational pattern is likely to be frustrated.

Some general goals are as follows:

1. Locate the stores as conveniently as possible for the consumer.

2. Present the consumer with a wide selection of goods by concentrating specialized goods in only a few stores.

3. Insure that each store has sufficient sales territory so that it can develop large enough sales volume to make a profit.

4. Separate stores that compete with one another but bring together stores of a complementary nature.

Such goals have little operational significance, especially if city administrators and city planners decree that new store construction in urban areas must be confined to the first floors of new apartment buildings (Serebriakov, 1956, p. 56).* This, of course, limits the size and scope of retail operations. With certain exceptions, this has meant that all new stores have been of a specialized nature.

The significance of a locational plan is affected not only by the restraints placed on new construction but also by the necessity of having to work with the Czarist trade network. Most of the larger stores in the Soviet Union were built on locations selected in the prerevolutionary era. The result is often the duplication of facilities and merchandise such as exists in Leningrad where Gostnyi Dvor and Passazh face each other across the street. In such circumstances, there are at least two obstacles confronting the marketing officials when they attempt to change an existing pattern. The most common difficulty is the cost involved in reoutfitting a building and moving equipment around. Another is that zoning laws designed to preserve historical traditions often preclude a more rational economic arrangement. For example, the resurrection of the central depart-

---

* The Russians seem to have led the United States in providing housing projects with shopping facilities; many early American projects were not provided with such conveniences.

ment store in the otherwise redeveloped and reorganized city of Volgagrad (Stalingrad) is explained by the fact that Marshal von Paulus surrendered in its basement. That this location is now inconvenient for shoppers in the new layout of the city was evidently considered to be of lesser importance (Alderson and Sessions, July, 1955, p. 3). Marketing officials in Leningrad are faced with the same type of problem (Goldman, 1959, p. 10).

Recently marketing officials have been allocated special construction resources, which have enabled them to give some meaning to their locational plans. The construction of a special building for children's goods, Detskii Mir (Children's World), in downtown Moscow and the prospective opening of a radically designed shopping center in the suburbs unattached to any apartment house indicate a more flexible approach to the problem of planned location. For that matter, while the use of first floors in new apartment projects has had drawbacks, it has been a beneficial policy in the sense that it has enabled marketing officials to move with the population. However, it has been an inadequate movement. The effect of low priorities and historical inflexibility in carrying out a planned location policy is indicated by the fact that whereas retail sales volume had increased by almost three times from 1940 to 1960, the network of stores had grown by less than 30 per cent. Moreover, while the planned norm of salesclerk's positions (*rabochii mest*) to every 1,000 urban inhabitants is 6.6, the actual ratio was 4 per 1,000 (*Sovetskaia Torgovlia,* June 2, 1960, p. 2; July 9, 1960, p. 1, July, 1961, p. 3; Skovoroda, Feb., 1960, p. 49). The persistence of this trend suggests the difficulties involved in implementing a locational pattern according to plan. In fact, it tends to imply that there may be no over-all locational plan and that stores are often opened up on the basis of day-to-day decisions.

Misallocation of Goods

As retail sales have continued to grow, some of the shortages of specific goods have been eliminated. Thus, failure to produce exactly as planned is no longer a crucial matter. Once this difficulty has been resolved, then a second type of problem arises—the proper allocation by marketing officials of a supply that is now fairly adequate. It should not be assumed that this has become the major problem—far from it. None the less, in the years following Stalin's death, one finds growing evidence of simultaneous gluts and deficits of the same goods. Even though there were abundant supplies in the warehouse, some stores were found to lack salt, shoes, kerosene, matches, fish, and socks. One area reported having received enough women's socks for ten years, but they were all one size. Flashlights were sent to one area, the batteries to another (Khrekin, Jan., 1959, p. 45; Khrekin, 1957, p. 6; *Sovetskaia Torgovlia,* Sept. 27, 1958, p. 2; *Kommunist Tadzhikistana,* Dec. 17, 1958, p. 3;. Khrushchev, *Pravda,* Oct. 8, 1959, p. 1, and *New York Times,* Dec. 27, 1959, p. 1; *Kommunist Tadzhikistana,* Mar. 25, 1958, p. 3; *Sovetskaia Kirgiziia,* Apr. 12, 1958, p. 3). The over-all supply of these goods in the country appears to be sufficient to meet aggregate demand, but more diligence in the process of allocation is necessary to satisfy specific needs.

Mistakes in interpreting planning data are wasteful under any circumstances. With central planning, the effect of a faulty decision may be greater because the decisions taken are usually on a broader scale. Even clerical errors are potentially more expensive. Since human beings not only gather the market data but also interpret them, the possibility of a mistake through neglect or lack of diligence cannot be ruled out on the grounds that under socialism a planned system is possible.

Such mistakes in the planning of Soviet retail trade may often have secondary and tertiary effects, which must be anticipated long in advance. For example, normally 40 per cent of the retail sales volume in Moscow is accounted for by out-of-town consumers (Khrekin, 1958, p. 20). As trade conditions have improved throughout the country, however, there has been somewhat less need to travel to Moscow to obtain hard-to-find goods. Failing to anticipate this, Moscow planners in 1956 overestimated 1956 retail sales. Because the available purchasing power in Moscow was insufficient to purchase the goods that had been made available, many of the goods had to be reshipped throughout the country.

Even simple situations may be handled poorly. There are at least two important cases in which the planner neglected to include television sets in the retail sales plans despite the opening of local television stations (*Sovetskaia Torgovlia*, June 11, 1959, p. 3; *Sovetskaia Moldavia*, Apr. 8, 1958, p. 3). In one instance, this situation persisted for three years. It must be emphasized that the transfer of decision-making powers to local authorities does not guarantee that simple mistakes will be avoided.

Unpredictability of the Consumer

Concern about estimating the supply of consumers' goods correctly and retaining flexibility in the allocation and distribution of those goods is only worth the effort if it is possible to predict consumption and demand. If demand is arbitrary and dimensionless, then much of the energy devoted to ascertaining agricultural output and allocation, as well as priorities for consumers' goods is wasted. This is not to deny that it may be worth while to plan agricultural and consumers'-goods output in the attempt to increase production per se. Yet if the commodities are not created in response to consumption desires and backed by financial resources of the prospective consumers, the emphasis on production for production's sake may have as much meaning as the full grain-storage warehouses in the American Midwest.

As the Edsel Division of the Ford Motor Company can testify, estimation of consumer demand is not always a simple matter. Though market research in Western countries continues to improve, a large measure of impression and unpredictability remains. As a theoretical matter, who has yet been able to measure individual or collective indifference curves on an operational basis? *

In the preceding pages of this chapter, it was suggested that the Soviets imply they have mastered these matters because of the planned nature of their system. Considering that the concepts of indifference curves and demand

---

* Until a recent paper by A. A. Konius (Pisarev, 1959, p. 181), the whole concept of indifference curves has been foreign to Soviet economic analysis. This is the first time to my knowledge that it has appeared in post-1930 Soviet writings.

elasticity are new or untested concepts in the Soviet Union, the Western observer may have legitimate doubts about any such mastery. To this writer's knowledge, there have been only a few empirical attempts in the Soviet Union to ascertain spending differences by income and cultural groups. One of the best is a remarkable budget study article by I. Korzhenevskii (Mar., 1959, p. 19). While the information collected by the Central Statistical Administration (TsSU) would indicate that other such studies are possible, there is little evidence that the budget material is used for this purpose. Generally, only the demand for such inelastic commodities as milk and bread is calculated. More important, the utilization of these techniques by trade planners seems negligible. Unless budget studies and other methods of market research are actually used by the trade planners, it would seem almost impossible to have an effective system of demand estimation even for goods for which the demand is inelastic.

As the standard of living improves, the problems of demand estimation become more complex.* In such cases, it is not the inability to rely on production goals or the human miscalculation of the planners that leads to misallocation; instead, the problem is that once the basic needs of the consumer have been satisfied and he has discretionary income at his disposal, his subsequent actions become more difficult to predict.

It must be emphatically emphasized that this is not as yet a typical condition. A visit to any Russian home or, for that matter, a walk down any Russian street is proof of that. Until a few years ago, there was little evidence of the

---

* For a discussion of how the standard of living has improved, see Goldman (July, 1960, p. 625).

inability to sell anything that had been producd. None the less, in the late 1950's growing complaints about gluts and surpluses began to appear. For the first time, there were no longer reports of offsetting deficits elsewhere. In a nationwide inventory climaxing the decade, it was found that inventories were several billion rubles in excess of the preplanned norms (Sapel'nikov, Dec., 1959, p. 3; *Sovet-skaia Torgovlia,* Sept. 1, 1960, p. 2; *Ekonomicheskaia Gazeta;* Dec. 25, 1961, p. 32). A glut, or overproduction, is taken to mean that, at the existing prices, already produced articles are not sold. Instead, goods remain on the shelves, and inventories soon exceed previous expectations. The Russians call this *zatovarovanie*. Specifically, there has been excess inventory formation of watches, bicycles, and expensive models of cameras, radios, and television sets (Khrekin, 1957, p. 6; Lisitsian, 1957, p. 17; *Novye Tovary,* June, 1961, p. 19; *Sovetskaia Torgovlia,* Dec., 1960, p. 15, Mar. 21, 1961, p. 2). Khrushchev highlighted the issue with his announcement at the Twenty-second Party Congress that shoe inventory had mounted to 1.5 billion rubles.

The simplest explanation for the appearance of overproduction in the "planned" Soviet economy is that for the first time the Soviet consumer is being given a choice in the selection of certain items. As production of consumers' goods gradually increases, it is not only a question of deciding between a camera or a television set, it is also necessary to choose between expensive makes of television sets. If measurement of consumer demand is to serve as a gauge of how to allocate television sets to retail outlets, it is now necessary to ascertain not only how many television sets will be demanded but also how many of a specific make and model.

Obviously it is only when the supply of a given commodity is increased, that the matter calls for any serious consideration:

> In the first years of the postwar period, our industry did not fully provide for the needs of the national economy. Consequently, the task of the marketing officials was concluded when the goods received were rapidly turned over to the consumer. Merchandise in this period did not lie idle and marketing personnel did not devote much attention to quality and assortment. They were not especially worried about their sales volume. But now, when our industry has produced consumer goods in sufficient quantity and in wide assortment, the role and task of workers in Soviet trade is sharply changed.
>
> . . . The problem is that in spite of a significant growth of production, consumer goods cannot satisfy the demands of the population if the people's demands are not studied and if that which the consumers need is not produced. Certainly it is one matter to produce goods in general, and another matter to produce that which the consumer demands (Amunov, Dec. 17, 1958, p. 3).

A concrete example of the problem was spelled out to me by A. I. Sobolev, formerly the assistant director of trade in Leningrad. "After the war, determining the demand for radios was no problem. At that time, we produced only five makes. Now, however, we produce and must determine the demand for twenty-five."

No longer is it simply a matter of determining the demand for bread and sugar, goods the Russians always cite when describing the process of demand estimation. For items like radios, which are purchased once every few years and for which the demand is more elastic, demand estimation becomes a more difficult task. When it is necessary to make long-range plans, even planning for a simple item like a man's shirt is not easy. If increased production means the consumer is to have a wider variety of choice, it is necessary to predict not only the correct assortment of sizes and fabric but such other variables as style of collar (plain, button-down, or sport) and color (white, blue, striped).

Even before the advent of buyer's market conditions, the matter of style became important. While it is possible to adjust to the secondary phases of a style cycle as long as the provincial areas adopt the style of Moscow and Leningrad, it seems considerably more difficult to predict just what the fickle consumers in Moscow and Leningrad are going to do in the first place. Having to make a decision a year in advance doesn't make the planner's job any easier, especially when the manufacturer may refuse to alter his outdated product mix (*Turkmenskaia Iskra,* July 23, 1959, p. 3).

As the variety, as well as the over-all quantity, of production increases, the scope for variation in taste is increased. Demand then truly becomes a function of all the factors mentioned earlier. Cultural and income differences and personal whim have a decided influence.

Since the Russians acknowledge the significance of all these variables, one should expect these factors to play a role in demand estimation studies. Unfortunately, innocent generalization about population differences in the socialist state does not mean the planners are making explicit recognition of the substantially unequal income and cultural categories. While wage differentials of almost thirty to one have existed in the Soviet Union, the printed acknowledgment of even a two-to-one differential is awkward ideologically. Moreover, while a member of the contemporary urban upper class would never for a second dispute the fact that his standard of living is culturally different from that of the rural peasant or even that of the urban lower class, it simply is not feasible to spell out specific classifications and differences in Soviet literature.

Occasionally, as in the previously cited article by Korzhenevskii (1959), one does find explicit recognition of such differences. But when Korzhenevskii argued that such studies are necessary if demand is to be properly estimated, he subjected himself to considerable risk. For his efforts, Korzhenevskii was attacked with the full force of Lenin and Khrushchev (Sapel'nikov, *et al.*, July, 1959. p. 25).* While many rationalizations were cited, the fact that it is embarrassing to admit the existence of widely differentiated income categories in a socialist state was doubtless the prime motive for the criticism. The challengers of Korzhenevskii also felt that such an approach to demand estimation would be difficult to implement. This would seem to be verified by a report in *Vestnik Statistiki,* which stated that a master plan of consumer demand measurement was introduced in 1953 and canceled the same year because of such difficulties (Tenenbaum, No. 3, 1954, pp. 21-22).

A further indication that the Soviets are still ill-equipped to carry on such work seems indicated by the fact that their dietary norms, as well as general household budget breakdowns, are apparently mere modifications of American standards and norms. The Research Institute of the

---

* Korzhenevskii's work has since been defended by A. Romanov, an assistant minister of trade in the Ukraine ("Sozdat' Nauchnuiu Metodiku Izucheniia Sprosa," *Sovetskaia Torgovlia,* May, 1960, p. 6). It is likely that the debate will continue.

Ministry of Trade (NIITOP—Naucho-Issledovatel'skie Institut Torgovli i Obshchestvennogo Pitaniia) has indicated to this author that their norms are based on the standards established in *The Nutritional Standards of the National Research Council of Nutritional Studies,* the series on food and agriculture edited by Fred C. Blanch, and *The World's Food* by M. K. Bennett, with "suitable" adjustments for the Russian character and climate. While this may be perfectly feasible, it would seem that such a procedure is subject to error.

In summary, it is certainly not argued that all is chaos in planning the distribution of consumers' goods in the Soviet Union. Goods do move through the channels sketched and do reach the consumer. What is suggested, however, is that the Soviet system apparently has not solved the basic planning problems of demand estimation and distribution that also perplex Western marketing authorities.

RECENT ATTEMPTS TO IMPROVE THE DISTRIBUTION PROCESS

In recognition that changes are needed to improve the allocation of consumers' goods, the government recently has introduced several reforms in the distribution process. As production of consumers' goods has increased, a central planning mechanism for these goods has become more difficult to operate. It may be perfectly possible to plan the share of national income to be directed to consumers' goods, but the task becomes increasingly more complicated as planning is forced to specify size, variety, and location of specific sales. This would then seem to be at least a partial explanation for the decentralization of the administrative structure described earlier. As expressed by one authority, "We had to stop the Moscow officials from telling the Vladivostok cooks how to make borsch" (Nefedov, July, 1958, p. 15).

Less reliance is being placed on central allocation in the form of funded and centrally planned categories of goods. Since 1957, an increasing number of goods have been distributed by means of direct contracts. Now a majority of the thousands of various consumers' goods are so allocated. Direct contracts providing for specific transactions not covered within the plan between wholesale and retail organizations and the factory and wholesale organizations have become more important. The result is considerably more flexibility and less bureaucratic interference. As pointed out earlier, the Ministry of Trade of the USSR was abolished and its all-Union planning work reduced and transferred to Soiuzglavtorg and Gosplan. Although the directors (as good bureaucrats) expect the scope of their organization to grow, the functions of Soiuzglavtorg will probably be concerned more with the allocation of investment funds for production of various consumers' goods rather than with the shipment of specific items.

If the process of distribution is to be conducted on a basis of direct contracts, some mechanism must be provided for linking up suppliers and recipients. In centralized planning this is all done in the offices of the Ministry of Trade or Gosplan. Clearly, some institutional arrangement is necessary to permit the same type of interchange in a more decentralized economy. To facilitate such contact, there has been a significant increase in the number of *iarmarki,* or trade fairs, held throughout the country. Here wholesale and retail organizations have a chance to bargain and match stocks and needs. Not only do local organizations participate, but trade representatives from all over the Soviet Union are invited to attend.

At least twice a year, there is a trade fair for each major line of goods. One such fair anticipated sales of about 300 million rubles of sports and cultural goods, 400 million rubles of household wares, and 700 million rubles of haberdashery. If such trade fairs are classified as being vertical-type fairs for specific items, there are also horizontal-type fairs held by the trade authorities of a certain city or *oblast.* The purpose here is to readjust existing stocks of various goods by selling commodities that one trade organization has in abundance to another that can put them to use. These fairs are sponsored by Trade Intermediary Agencies (*Torgovo Posrednicheskoi*) for three or four days at a time. Monthly business-trend circulars and catalogs (*kon'iuktory obzor*) describing surplus stocks and trade conditions are prepared and distributed. Sales volume may run into several hundred million rubles, although usually it is less.

The trade fair convened in Moscow during January, 1961, was one of the most significant and impressive of all such fairs. It could be described as both horizontal and vertical. It was a nationwide fair with considerable advance publicity. Participants included not only wholesalers but retailers and manufacturers of all varieties of food products. Not only were unsalable goods exchanged between wholesalers, but brand new goods were also offered for sale. Sales volume amounted to 10.4 billion rubles with another 100 million rubles worth of goods unsold. (Unsold goods were primarily those products that had already been sitting on shelves for some time.)

There are other ramifications connected with decentralization. Wholesalers advertise their needs and surpluses. Occasionally one even finds references to traveling salesmen. Further, as sellers' markets abate, quality becomes more important and consumer acceptance begins to assume a significance similar to that in a Western economy (Goldman, 1960, p. 346).

CONCLUSION

In conclusion it has been argued that as production of consumers' goods grows, centralized planning of their production and distribution becomes increasingly difficult. While broad decisions as to the percentage of national income to be invested on consumption may still be retained at the top of the pyramid, more flexibility is required in the distribution of specific commodities. The nature of the raw materials, as well as the priority the state planners have accorded to consumers' goods, has always made the allocative planning of consumers' goods more difficult than planning in heavy industry. Furthermore, as more goods become available, it becomes more difficult to make centralized demand estimates. Miscalculations seem inevitable, with excess inventory formation and surpluses the result. In turn, this leads to decentralization and increased market activity.

It is not to be implied, by any means, that buyer's market conditions for all consumers' goods have suddenly developed in the Soviet Union. Yet there have been some indications of such a change in the market conditions for certain commodities and a gradual improvement in the availability of almost all lines. What has been emphasized here is the trend toward a more demanding consumer. Given such a trend, Soviet experience seems to show that more reliance must be placed on decentralized, rather than centralized, decision-making.

[4] *PRICING OF CONSUMERS' GOODS*

INTRODUCTION

THE QUESTION of pricing in the Soviet Union is a complex and controversial matter. Even though there has always been considerable discussion among Soviet economists concerning the role and meaning of prices, the death of Stalin, the subsequent intellectual thaw, and the drive for efficiency in a rapidly maturing industrial economy produced an intensification of the debate (various issues of *Voprosy Ekonomiki,* beginning with No. 2, 1957, and continuing until at least Aug., 1958; Kulikov, No. 8, 1958, p. 90; Tsagolov, 1959; Kronrod, 1959).

Essentially, there seem to be two major issues in the Soviet debate about pricing: (1) the relationship of price to demand and its effect on the efficient functioning of the market, and (2) the relationship of price to cost and its effect on the efficient allocation of resources. While all the ramifications of the pricing controversy are most interesting, in a study of marketing it seems proper to focus primarily on the first issue, which is of more concern to distribution officials. Once this is done there will be a description of the organizations whose job it is to determine Russian prices. Finally, Marx's attitude toward pricing will be contrasted with Soviet practice.

THE NATURE OF RETAIL PRICES

Price formation of consumers' goods in the Soviet Union generally involves the determination of prices at two levels: the wholesale price of the manufacturer as the goods leave his premises (*optovaia tsena predpriiatiia*) and the final retail price as the goods are placed on the shelf by the ultimate seller. These two prices are normally the only ones officially approved and published. Other intermediary prices are not determined independently but are derived by subtracting components of the retail price from the total retail price. (See Figure 5.)

The first aspect of the Soviet pricing process to be examined is what determines the final retail price and to what extent this final price is affected by demand considerations. The most notable feature about the retail price is that it is usually double the wholesale price of the manufacturing firm. About 20 per cent of this increment is accounted for by costs of distribution and a small figure for planned profit. The remainder of the increment is called a "turnover tax."

Prior to 1949, an explicit rate of turnover tax existed for each type of goods. When this rate was applied to the wholesale price of the manufacturer, the result was the final retail price. Under such conditions the pricing process focused on the determination of the turnover tax rate, not

Figure 5—The Structure of Retail Prices

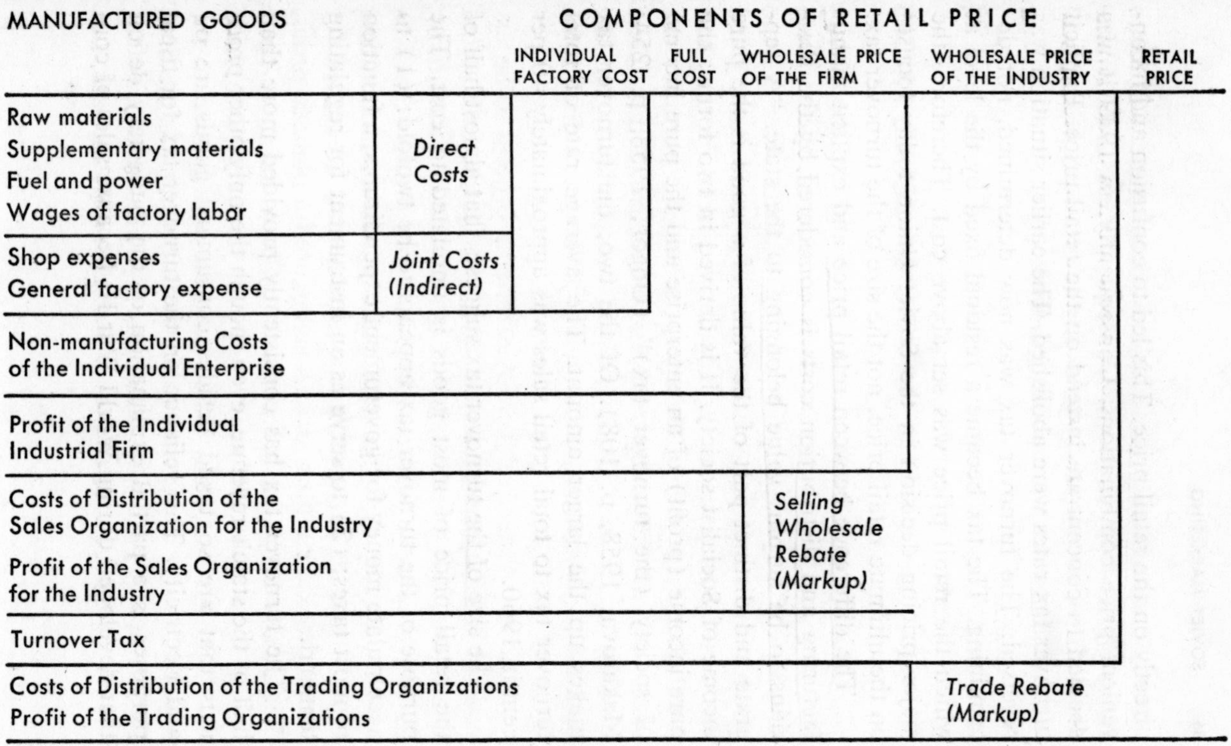

COMPONENTS OF RETAIL PRICE

MANUFACTURED GOODS	INDIVIDUAL FACTORY COST	FULL COST	WHOLESALE PRICE OF THE FIRM	WHOLESALE PRICE OF THE INDUSTRY	RETAIL PRICE
Raw materials / Supplementary materials / Fuel and power / Wages of factory labor	Direct Costs				
Shop expenses / General factory expense	Joint Costs (Indirect)				
Non-manufacturing Costs of the Individual Enterprise					
Profit of the Individual Industrial Firm					
Costs of Distribution of the Sales Organization for the Industry					
Profit of the Sales Organization for the Industry			Selling Wholesale Rebate (Markup)		
Turnover Tax					
Costs of Distribution of the Trading Organizations					
Profit of the Trading Organizations					Trade Rebate (Markup)

SOURCE: Lifits, 1955, p. 441.

directly on the retail price. This led to confusion and inconvenient price combinations. Consequently, in 1949 it was decided to concentrate instead on the retail price. Explicit turnover tax rates were abolished. The earlier situation was reversed. The turnover tax was now determined, not determining. The tax became a residual fixed by the level at which the retail price was set above cost. Therefore, the major pricing decision in the Soviet Union today focuses on the ultimate retail price, not the size of the turnover tax.

The difference between retail price and explicit manufacturing and distribution costs is considered by the Russians to be surplus value belonging to the state. "A separate and distinct part of the value of a good is the pure income of Socialist society. It is derived in two forms: the pure income (profit) of an enterprise and the pure income of society (the turnover tax)" (Gogol', 1958, p. 254; Makarova, 1958, p. 108). Of the two, the turnover tax makes up the larger amount. The average rate of total turnover tax to total retail sales was approximately 40 per cent in 1960.

The size of the turnover tax suggests that almost half of the retail price of most goods is unrelated to cost. The purpose of the turnover tax appears to be twofold: (1) to accumulate money for government expenditures, a function of most taxes; (2) to serve as an instrument for regulating demand.

The turnover tax has consistently provided more than half of the state's revenue, even though the only other products that are so taxed besides consumers' goods are oil and electricity. This reliance on the turnover tax for fiscal purposes is a partial explanation of the budgetary deficit that developed during World War II. Because sales of consumers' goods fell sharply, there were no tax receipts to collect.

Of particular relevance to this chapter, however, is the significant role the turnover tax plays as a regulator of demand. Soviet economists frankly recognize this to be one of the main tasks of the turnover tax (Makarova, 1958, p. 123; A. Kulikov, No. 8, 1958, p. 106; *Voprosy Ekonomiki,* Feb., 1959, pp. 104-5; Speech by I. A. Mikoyan, *Kommunist,* Mar. 12, 1958, p. 1; Bukh, 1959, pp. 50-51). It is used both to restrain and to stimulate demand. In the first instance, this may be a response to general inflationary pressures or a reflection of a moral attitude; in the second case, it may indicate an intentional subsidy for a particular population group or a desire to reduce inventories.

Because of the emphasis devoted to the heavy industrial sector, one of the most pressing tasks in the Russian economy has been to mop up the large amounts paid out in wages for which there exists no equivalent fund of consumers' goods. If the standard of living is low, failure to absorb excessive purchasing power in an economy where prices reflect only production and distribution costs will be manifested by queues, private resale of goods, and inflationary prices for goods on the *kolkhoz* market. Since the problem of balancing purchasing power and available supplies has not always been resolved successfully, it has been necessary to ration the available goods by means of substantial price increments above cost. The main task of the price-maker, therefore, is to establish a retail price that will absorb as much of the excess purchasing power as possible and create a balance between supply and demand.

An analysis of the inflationary pressures that were especially strong in the early thirties and forties has been presented by Franklyn Holzman (May, 1960, pp. 167, 171).* By comparing the relationship of *kolkhoz* market prices to prices in the government and cooperative stores, he traces the existence of unsatisfied purchasing power. If there is an increase or decrease in purchasing power unaccompanied by a corresponding change in the supply of consumers' goods or their prices in the government and cooperative stores, this will be indicated by a rise or fall in *kolkhoz* market prices. Since the latter is only indirectly regulated by the state, it is a good index of inflationary or deflationary pressure.

While the turnover tax has been used in past years to reduce some of the demand potential, prior to 1947 it had been only partially successful. None the less, if government and cooperative store prices had reflected cost elements only, the queues would have been longer, the shelves emptier, and the prices in the *kolkhoz* market higher.

After the 1947 monetary reform, much of the excessive inflationary tension of the past was eliminated, and the effectiveness of the turnover tax as a regulator of demand was improved. To provide a better balance between supply and demand, official retail prices were increased as a result of the reform and approximately 90 per cent of the outstanding currency was destroyed.

The effectiveness of the 1947 reform is proved by the fact that subsequently it was possible to introduce a series of price cuts. In fact, annual price reductions were made from 1948 to 1954, which resulted in lower prices not only in government and cooperative stores but in the *kolkhoz* market.

However, while conditions have improved, Table 8 sug-

---

* Conditions were even worse in the period of War Communism (Makarova, May, 1960, p. 120).

gests that an inflationary gap still exists. While partly a reflection of higher quality, *kolkhoz* market prices remain over 35 per cent higher than the same prices in government and cooperative stores. The result is that there are still many undesirable situations in which prices do not provide a smooth distribution of goods. In some instances, moreover, the price reductions went too far. It was acknowledged that prices of certain goods were no longer high enough to offset demand pressures adequately. Accordingly, prices were raised in 1958 on such items as sewing machines, automobiles, refrigerators, and fruit (Kronrod, 1959, pp. 385-86; *Pravda,* Jan. 2, 1958, p. 1; *Sovetskaia Rossiia,* Jan. 3, 1958, p. 1). Apparently they were not raised enough, since demand still seems to exceed the supply at the existing prices. Illicit resale of certain goods still occurs. Black markets for automobiles flourish, and special laws have been enacted to prevent people from signing up again and again for automobiles with the intention of reselling them (*Sovetskaia Litva,* May 22, 1958, p. 2; *Sovetskaia Estonia,* Jan. 7, 1958, p. 3; *Turkmenskaia Iskra,* Dec. 17, 1957, p. 3).* The humiliating 25 per cent increase in the price of meat and butter on June 1, 1962, is further evidence that the Russians have not perfected their techniques of price formation.

High turnover tax rates and higher prices are used not only to curtail demand when supplies are short but are also often applied when, although supplies are abundant, consumption of the particular product is considered undesirable. A high excise tax is imposed on the consumption of alcoholic beverages, tobacco, and such luxury items as jewelry and precious stones. While consumption is dis-

---

* It would seem that the Soviet economic system does not necessarily respond to long lines by increasing production as it increases prices.

Table 8—Relationship of Comparable Food Prices of Government and Cooperative Stores to Kolkhoz Markets (Selected Quarters and Yearly Averages) and Price Movements on the Kolkhoz Markets

Period	Kolkhoz Market Prices as Percentage of Government and Cooperative Stores	Kolkhoz Market Price Index (1954 Equals 100)
1954		
2nd quarter	170	
4th quarter	184	
Year	n.a.	100
1955		
2nd quarter	184	
4th quarter	159	
Year	n.a.	102
1956		
2nd quarter	152	
4th quarter	132	
Year	145 *	91
1957		
2nd quarter	136	
4th quarter	134	
Year	134	89
1958		
2nd quarter	142	
4th quarter	129	
Year	138	96
1959		
2nd quarter	134	
4th quarter	127	
Year	131	92
1960		
2nd quarter	141	
4th quarter	130	
Year	135	97

SOURCE: Derived from data found in TsSU 6, pp. 133, 134, 183; TsSU 3, pp. 773, 774, 790; TsSU 5, pp. 718, 719, 738.

* It will be noted that Holzman tends to overstate the degree of inflation for this year in the *Quarterly Journal of Economics*, May, 1960, p. 169.

couraged to some extent, the inelastic nature of the demand for some of these products suggests that a high turnover tax on such goods is also a profitable fiscal weapon.

While a higher turnover tax can be used to reduce

demand, a lower turnover tax will increase it. Occasionally, prices are intentionally set below the level at which demand meets supply. This often implies that the turnover tax rate on some goods is lower than on others. In fact, for some products there is little or no turnover tax. It is claimed that some consumers' goods occasionally are even sold below cost. Prices of books and children's items, such as clothing, shoes, and school supplies, are deliberately priced low to enable lower income groups to purchase them. Although the turnover tax on some basic consumption products is low and on some luxury items is high, there is no evidence to indicate that basic consumption needs are necessarily taxed at a low rate. For example, the turnover tax rate for basic, nonstylized adult shoes is approximately 35–37 per cent of the retail price. While this may be below the over-all average turnover tax rate, it still is unusually high.

In addition to reducing prices and turnover taxes on goods consumed by particular population groups, the state may adjust prices and turnover taxes to encourage or discourage the consumption of some products in a given locality. While the prices of some goods are uniform throughout the Soviet Union, the prices of other goods are varied according to whether or not they are sold in urban or rural areas and whether or not they are in Zone I or Zone III of a nationwide system of price zones.

In the discussion of the cooperative trade system in Chapter 2, it was pointed out that a 7 per cent premium was required for a wide assortment of goods sold in rural areas. Since usually no more than a 0.5 per cent markup is required to pay for the additional transportation expense, the remainder of the 7 per cent premium often represents a form of rural taxation on the peasants and an attempt to curtail some of their demand (Kolosovskii and Rozen-blium, 1958, p. 38).

In zonal pricing, an attempt is made to take into account availability of supply and cost of transportation. The base zone, or Zone I, is usually defined as an important production area for the particular goods. Consequently, a given area may be in Zone I for one item, and in the higher-priced Zone III for another. (See Table 9.) Before the war, there were four to eight zones, but now there are three for most products. The third zone usually encompasses the North and Far East, where production of consumers' goods is smallest and transportation cost greatest.

As a result of zonal pricing, the level of prices varies significantly between different areas of the Soviet Union. Recently prices were 7 per cent higher in Moscow than in the southern part of the country and 10 per cent higher in the republics of Latvia, Lithuania, and Estonia than in Central Asia and Kazakhstan (Bukhanevich and Sonin, Jan., 1957, p. 26). In Siberia and the far northern regions, all prices were 16 per cent higher than in other more favorably located areas.

Table 9—Price Classification for Various Areas and Commodities

Republic, Krai, or Oblast	ZONE				
	Bread Products	Confectionery Products	Fish	Lumber Materials	Window Glass
Moscow *Oblast*	II	II	II	II	I
Republic of Georgia	II	II	II	VI	I
Republic of Uzbekstan	I	I	I	VII	II
Khabarovskii *Krai*	III	III	I	n.a.	II

SOURCE: Kulikov and Smotrina, 1959, p. 11.

While zonal differences undoubtedly are a partial reflection of transportation and production cost differences, they also are a function of demand pressures. Goods in the Far North are often in reduced supply relative to the high salaries in the area. In recognition of this, retail prices and, in effect, turnover tax rates are manipulated so that varying prices and tax rates apply for the same goods in different areas. Thus, in Table 9 the prices of all goods, except fish and perhaps lumber, are higher in Khabarouskii Krai than in the central areas of the country. This helps to explain why prices in the Far North and Siberia—that is, in Belts 4 and 5—are at least 16 per cent higher than in the rest of the country.

It is not only because of scarcity that prices are manipulated. This can be seen in Table 9, where it is indicated that bread and confectionery products in Uzbekstan are priced at the lower, Zone I prices. Even though the basic crop in Uzbekstan is cotton and little food is harvested, food prices are lower there than in other more favorably located regions like Moscow. From this example it can be seen that the turnover tax can be used not only to encourage the demand for certain specific items in abundant supply, but also to influence production. By subsidizing food prices in Uzbekstan, the government discourages the peasants from growing their own food. Since food is priced at relatively low prices, the peasants tend to concentrate on growing cotton. Therefore, by variations in the turnover tax and, through it, in the final retail price, the government is able to stimulate not only consumption but production. Furthermore, the low price of wheat in Uzbekstan suggests that zonal pricing need not always reflect differences in cost.

As over-all production has increased and inventories of various goods have begun to exceed preplanned limits, the turnover tax has become an especially important weapon in stimulating demand. In Chapter 3, it was shown that the problem of overstocked inventories is becoming increasingly serious. If it is determined that supply exceeds demand at the existing price for a given television set, Soviet authorities recognize that one solution is to lower prices. (*Kommunist,* Mar. 12, 1958, p. 2; Mikoyan, May, 1958, pp. 1-4). Consequently, there have been a series of specific price reductions on such items since 1956, as opposed to the broad price cuts on almost all consumers' goods during the years 1948-1954 (*Pravda,* Jan. 2, 1958, p. 1, and July 1, 1959, p. 5; *Sovetskaia Torgovlia,* Aug. 4, 1958, p. 4, and March 1, 1960, p. 1).

The use of reduced prices to stimulate demand can be achieved not only by altering the turnover tax but also by adjustment of the profit rate. Retail trade organizations are now required to set aside a fixed percentage of their annual retail sales in order to compensate for periodic markdowns of goods. Beginning in January, 1960, instead of being counted as profit, 0.2 per cent of retail sales volume was to be used to make up the difference on the sales of goods at prices lower than originally anticipated. Because this proved inadequate, the figure was raised to 0.4 per cent in September, 1960 (*Sovetskaia Torgovlia,* Mar. 17, 1960, p. 4, and Sept. 1, 1960, p. 2; Lifits, Nov., 1959, p. 108). By lowering prices on end-of-season leftovers, it was hoped to reduce inventories and the accumulation of shopworn goods by an intentional stimulation of demand through lowered prices.

The manipulation of seasonal prices offers a convenient illustration of all the techniques discussed above. In a short time sequence, prices are used first to restrain and then to encourage demand. The price pattern of Moscow tomatoes in the summer of 1959 is a typical example of this. In cognizance of the necessity for demand restraint while supplies were scarce, the price of a kilogram of tomatoes until July 13 was 2 rubles. On July 23, as the supplies increased, the price was lowered to 1 ruble. It was expected that the price would be decreased to 70 or 80 kopecks before the end of the month (Goldman, 1959, p. 28). While a price reduction of more than 60 per cent within one month's time may suggest a volatility exceeding that to be expected from sophisticated planners, it certainly indicates an awareness of the effect of seasonal production on supply and demand conditions.

To sum up, it has been shown that demand pressures are an important consideration in Soviet pricing policy. This is primarily manifested through manipulation of the turnover tax, although other price components may be utilized. This is not to say that Soviet retail pricing reflects the forces of demand in the same way that prices do in the United States.* Moreover, a better adjustment is apparently made on some items than on others. Yet the fact remains that the retail price is established at a considerably higher level than the explicit costs arising from production and distribution. The determination by the planner of how much he should add to the price of a specific product above and beyond its costs is partly a reflection of the demand pressures for that item. Consequently, demand is a basic component of the retail price and is recognized as such by the Russians.

---

* For that matter, even United States prices after World War II were often held below otherwise possible levels; for example, prices on automobiles in 1946.

THE PRICE-MAKERS AND THEIR PRICES

To complete the description of retail pricing in the Soviet Union, it seems necessary to mention the price-making agencies and their authority. As it might be assumed, the determination of prices in the Soviet Union is an important power and one closely controlled by the central government authorities. In recent years, however, there has been considerable delegation of authority to republic and local officials.

Until 1957, retail prices on almost 80 per cent of all consumers' goods were determined at the upper administrative levels (Lifits, 1955, p. 436; Lopatkin, Mar., 1954, p. 79). As in the allocation process, the more important the government considers the commodity to be, the higher in the chain of command any decisions affecting it are taken. Prices for the most important goods are determined at an all-Union level. The Council of Ministers of the USSR is the final authority on such prices. However, the background data and the actual decisions are generally prepared and made by such subordinate units as Gosplan of the USSR, the Ministry of Trade, and occasionally by the Ministry of Finance.*

The task of establishing prices is not a simple one. While the problem of properly relating the price of one type of good to another is complicated enough, the gov-

---

* Iu. Zhukov says that the Ministry of Finance is involved only when the decision affects the *skidki* (rebates) ("Ob Uchebnykh Posobiiakh Po Kursu Ekonomiki Sovetskoi Torgovli," *Sovetskaia Torgovlia,* May, 1960, p. 34).

ernment price-makers are also responsible for maintaining certain price relationships between different areas in the country. As was mentioned above, the price-setters may decree a price differential between all urban and rural areas, or they may divide the country into price zones. Moreover, within a given zone, the prices may also be varied. In some cases, this represents the difference between urban and rural prices, and in other cases, it may be an extension of the over-all policy of pricing according to demand pressures and transportation expense (Skvortsov, Apr., 1957, p. 116). In addition to price variation because of geography, there are also price differences due to product heterogeneity and seasonal fluctuation. The difficulty involved in maintaining centralized price lists and the complexity arising from such a system can be easily envisaged when it is pointed out, for example, that at one time there were as many as 6,600 prices for various fish products (Gogol', 1957, p. 29).

As the production of consumers' goods has expanded, new products have been introduced. This has made the formation of prices and their relationships even more intricate. Naturally enough under such circumstances, pricing problems develop with ramifications extending beyond the field of pricing into planning and allocation.

Distortions in the prospective allocation plan often result because prices, costs, and profit incentives have not been carefully related to each other. For example, the fact that rebates (*skidki*) vary on different models of a particular product may produce unintended effects. Thus, in a seller's market the manager is usually interested in procuring those particular models that will provide him with the highest ruble rebate. Frequently this means the consumer will be shown only those goods with a high rebate and will be denied the opportunity of choosing from a well-balanced selection of goods. (For the type of problem involved, see Riauzov and Titel'baum, 1956, p. 191; Gatovskii, 1955, p. 71.)

Difficulties are also likely to arise because planning officials are often unable to foresee all the effects of their decisions. Ideally, prices should be established so that resulting price interactions do not create unintended and harmful effects. The possibility of making a faulty decision is especially great when price-setting power is concentrated in the hands of only a few officials who must foresee all the consequences of their decisions. For example, failure to anticipate all the implications led pricing officials to decree that prices on both sewn goods and unsewn goods would be reduced by the same percentage. There are many situations in which this would be an acceptable practice and no complications would arise. In this particular instance, however, the fabric prices should have been lowered by a larger percentage to allow for the decrease in the price of the finished dresses. Arbitrarily reducing the fabric and dress prices by the same amount made the sale of the dresses unprofitable (Kondrashev, 1956, p. 163).* Perceptive planners must anticipate these relationships. Yet, because there are often an infinite number of such interconnections, it is generally impossible to eliminate such errors.

As the variety of products produced has grown, the number of such problems has increased. It has become increasingly difficult to price all consumers' goods from a central location in Moscow. Because price relationships at

---

* Assume dresses sell for 80 rubles, fabric costs 50 rubles and labor used in making the dresses cost 25 rubles. If the prices of the dress and fabric are both lowered 20 per cent, instead of an initial profit of 5 rubles there will be a loss of 1 ruble.

lower levels are usually less complex and because local officials are frequently more familiar with practical operating problems, it was decided in March, 1957, to decentralize the price-making procedure for approximately 45 per cent of the consumers' goods sold through government and cooperative stores. The official power to approve prices on low priority and locally produced goods was delegated to government organizations at the republic, *oblast,* and city level. In all cases, ultimate authority was transferred to the general government group; that is, to the republic council of ministers, *sovnarkhoz, oblast* executive committee (*oblispolkom*), and even the city executive committee (*gorispolkom*). In effect, this meant that the act itself was delegated to operational planning units at the republic and local level, such as Gosplan or agencies of the ministry of trade.

To simplify further the price-making process, it was decided to eliminate many of the arbitrary price variations. Accordingly, some rural-urban distinctions were abolished. In 1958 and 1959, prices of jam and wine were made the same in rural and urban areas, and on January 1, 1960, the price differential on the sale of matches, soap, kerosene, perfume, stockings, and haberdashery products was abolished. The rural premium remains, however, on such items as sugar, confectionery products, fabrics, underwear, and shoes (Kolosovskii and Rozenblium, 1958, p. 32). Similarly, major differences persist despite an over-all lessening of zonal price differences.

Decentralization has made possible the simplification and elimination of many pricing difficulties; none the less, decentralization creates its own problems. When a particular republic or *oblast* has the power to establish the prices for products produced by its manufacturing firms, there is a possibility that several different retail prices will exist for the same type of goods. If consumers' goods are priced according to the usual method of FOB destination, differences in delivery prices may result as long as the product is produced under two different jurisdictions and two different sets of cost conditions. Such a situation complicates matters if distribution is to be by planned quota. Differential pricing easily creates counterpressures as the trade organizations seek their sources of supply from the most inexpensive producers rather than from the ones designated by the plan. To cope with this situation, the council of ministers of the receiving republic was authorized in 1959 to alter the prices of the shipping organization so that price differentials on the same product would not exist.

Moreover, although there may be more flexibility, decentralization does not guarantee that the local republic or *oblast* authorities will be able to determine prices any more effectively than the officials in Moscow (Skvortsov, June, 1958, pp. 71-72). Training and a certain degree of sophistication are necessary. While central government officials in Moscow may be unable to respond to local conditions, at least there is a stronger likelihood that they have had better technical training than local officials. Criticisms have already been heard that the pricing practices of the local authorities sometimes create more confusion than before *(Sovetskaia Torgovlia,* Oct. 22, 1959, p. 4; "Khronika-Soveshchanie po Tsenam," *Sovetskaia Torgovlia,* July, 1958, p. 7).

Thus, while control of the price system provides the planner with an important aid in implementing his goals, there is always the danger that prices will be incorrectly determined. This may result in counterpressures that offset other planning stimuli. The attempt to decentralize the price formation process with the aim of obtaining a more responsive price system may solve some of the problems, but it may lead, in turn, to new ones.

SOVIET PRICING IN RELATION
TO MARXIST THEORY

The final question that will be examined in connection with pricing in the Soviet Union is how actual practice corresponds with Marxist theory. From what has been said above, there is already considerable reason to suspect there may be substantial differences between theory and practice.

According to Marx, the basis of all value is labor. Only labor expended in the direct production of the goods or in the indirect labor embodied in the instruments and raw materials used for production creates real value. Marx allowed for varying degrees of skill and acknowledged that the value of work performed in one hour by a skilled worker and a common laborer is not the same. Nonetheless, the basic principle remained that a product is exchanged for another in direct proportion to the amount of socially necessary labor required for each.

What most disturbed Marx, however, was that the value of the goods produced always exceeded the pure labor value of both direct and embodied labor and the difference was retained by the capitalist. This was the inevitable result, since the employer had only to pay the laborer the value of his subsistence in return for which the laborer consigned his labor power to the employer. Since the value of subsistence was generally less than value produced by the worker in the course of a day, the employer emerged with a residue. This difference Marx called "surplus value." The fact that the capitalist and other members of the ruling upper classes appropriated this for themselves instead of for society as a whole was bitterly resented by Marx.

As was pointed out in Chapter 1, Marx did not limit his criticism to surplus value. To the extent that labor was employed in certain unapproved and socially unnecessary marketing and distribution activities, Marx refused to consider this labor expense as a true component of value. For example, the wages paid warehousemen for storing goods in an attempt to corner the market did nothing to increase real value. Although Marx admitted that warehousemen who placed certain perishable items under cover for reasons of protection sometimes performed a socially useful service, he felt that most other employees in service industries added little to value.

Anything that resulted in excessive transfer of title or affected price because of artificial scarcity would not be considered a legitimate value determinant. In fact, Marx had ruled out all demand factors in the consideration of value. Basing his theory on the ideas of the classical economists of his day, Marx felt that when demand did affect price, it was only because of manipulation, which did not change the real value of the goods. Perhaps if Alfred Marshall had demonstrated his two-bladed demand-and-supply scissors in Marx's youth, Marx would have had somewhat different ideas about value. As it was, labor to Marx was the only factor that could create value and did so only when it was socially useful. Land, capital, and most service functions, if they did contribute to value, did so only indirectly when they represented socially useful labor that had been embodied at an earlier stage.

In actuality, while the cost of labor, both direct and indirect, is the most important component in Soviet retail pricing practice, Russian economists consider that other economic factors make a contribution to value as well. Although there appears to be no explicit inclusion of an interest charge for fixed assets, store rent and interest on working capital are looked upon as legitimate costs of distribution. As will be shown in Chapter 7, they are also accounted for in the selling price.

Moreover, some labor expense that Marx would probably have considered socially unnecessary is included in cost as labor value. For example, advertising expense, although a relatively small figure, is considered to be a proper cost of distribution. The Soviet theorists justify this position with the claim that Soviet advertising is of an informative nature and therefore contributes to real value. The fact that some Soviet advertising is becoming increasingly competitive does not affect their reasoning. The same theoretical justification is made about storage. In theory it cannot be acknowledged that Soviet marketing personnel store goods for an excessive period of time, although in practice this happens. Consequently, storage costs are included in the price of goods regardless of the fact that such expense sometimes results from costly irrational and unplanned storage mistakes. In much the same manner, the expense of running the trade bureaucracy is considered a proper expense item even though there are numerous complaints about the waste such activities generate.

As for the effect of surplus value on value and price,

it was seen earlier how the Russians sanctioned the use of profits and turnover taxes as a means of capturing extra revenue for the state. From the Soviet point of view, this is an improvement over the capitalistic system, in which the residual is appropriated by the individual capitalist. However, while these two financial instruments doubtless serve as an important source of monetary accumulation for society as a whole, it is not so clear that they are applied at a uniformly proportional rate on all goods as sound labor value theory requires. It will be remembered that there is no turnover tax applied to most industrial goods. Moreover, the effective rates that apply to consumers' goods are not levied at a consistent rate. To the extent that the turnover tax rate for a particular good is determined by its peculiar demand considerations, it seems clear that a uniform rate of surplus value does not prevail. The inclusion in the price of rent and interest on working capital all but makes it impossible for the price of goods to be proportional to their embodied labor. Thus, it is unlikely that prices reflect value as defined by Marx.

CONCLUSION

The problems of pricing are complex in any society. With the power to control all the prices in a state concentrated in a few hands, it might seem possible for Russian price-makers to create a perfectly controlled system. Actually it turns out that the pricing interrelationships are so intricate that central price-makers are unable to anticipate all the side effects. Moreover, as the economy develops, the functions of the pricing system change and new problems develop. The pressures created by excess purchasing power have now been substantially reduced. With inflation no longer such a serious problem and with production of consumers' goods increasing, the role of the turnover tax as a check on demand is less important. Rather, as inventories have started to accumulate, it has been found necessary to readjust prices so that they encourage demand. Finally, although manipulation of the over-all turnover tax and profit rate to cope with particular demand conditions is likely to result in a more effective pricing system, it all but rules out adherence to the Marxist theory of value. The conclusion seems to be that the dictates of an effective pricing system preclude the complete acceptance of Marxist value theory.

[5] *FINANCIAL CONTROL*

INTRODUCTION

WHILE PLANNING in terms of physical units may be the more important operational and control method in Soviet trade and distribution, financial planning also plays an essential role. Financial planning affects almost every monetary transaction of the distribution enterprises. A plan is drawn up for all enterprises and organizations in which a predetermined profit is assigned, a timetable for the issuance of credit is outlined, and the flow of receipts and expenditures is scheduled and regulated. By means of any one of these controls, the present operating efficiency of a firm can be compared with that of the past or with other firms or with a plan. Armed with such procedures, the state, through both the ministry of trade and the banking system (Gosbank), is better able to supervise and operate its distibution system.

Financial planning in the distribution system is also the keystone in the monetary functioning of the economy. Since 90 per cent of the cash receipts entering Gosbank are deposited by the trade network and restaurants, it seems clear that any malfunctioning of the distribution network will not only affect the realized markup and profit accumulation of the retail and wholesale enterprise, but also the availability of cash resources throughout the whole Soviet Union (Tiukov, 1959, p. 5).

Financial planning and control is therefore important to both the distribution and trade authorities who control the operation of their subordinate units and to the state banking authorities. After an examination of the financial plan and the special significance of profit to Soviet marketing authorities, the nature of credit in trade and how it is used by the state bank to exercise control will be discussed.

THE FINANCIAL PLAN

At the firm level, the financial plan is mainly concerned with the firm's cash inflow and outflow. The latter includes wages, utility services, payment of supplier's bills, and bank loans. As in Western economies, the goal of the financial plan in Soviet enterprises is to take in as much money as possible above expenses in order to accumulate a profit.

The principle of *khozraschet,* or financial accounting, in the Soviet Union is substantially different, however, from the accounting concept of profit and loss in the West. While one of the main functions of a financial statement in the Soviet Union, as in other economies, is to provide an index of efficiency for the use of the administrative hierarchy, the meaning of profit is different. Even though profit in the Soviet Union represents the difference between revenue and expenses, a planned profit is arbitrarily assigned to the firm long in advance. It is expected that an efficiently operating firm will net its profit quota. It is only when revenue exceeds expense by a sum greater than the pre-determined planned profit that anything resembling profit in the capitalist sense is forthcoming. This means that at government-established prices and costs, the firm is efficient enough to earn more money than had been anticipated.

Despite this difference in approach, Russian profit, as in the United States, is the residual between revenue and expenditure. In the field of distribution, however, the revenue that is used in the profit calculation is not gross revenue but a percentage rebate (*skidka*) from the retail sales price of the goods. The rebates are totaled up, and the ruble equivalent is transferred to the firm as its operating revenue. The only expenditure subtracted from this is the cost of distribution; the wholesale price of the goods sold plus the turnover tax does not enter into the profit calculation of the retail enterprise. Thus, while the retail price consists of the wholesale price of the goods, the turnover tax, and the rebate, it is only the rebate that concerns the retailer. (See Figure 5.) It is from the rebate that he is supposed to cover his costs of distribution and make a profit.

In a sense, the rebate is equivalent to our percentage markup except that it is an amount deducted from the retail price. (Our custom is to add the markup to the wholesale price.) Table 10 shows selected rebates for a variety of goods and locations. Notice that the rebates are differentiated according to type of goods (20 per cent for salt, 3 per cent for cotton fabrics) and geography (3 per cent for cotton fabrics in the city, 12 per cent in the Far North). While more remote distribution outlets are given a higher rebate to cover increased transportation and storage costs, it should be remembered that variations in rebates are not necessarily related to variations in price. Thus, while Table

Table 10—Trade Rebates (Skidki) as a Per Cent of Retail Price

Product	City	Village	Distant and Mountain Regions	FAR NORTH, ETC.		
				City	Village	Special
Bread and bread products	6.5	6.5	6.5	6.5	6.5	6.5
Sugar	5.0	5.7	6.7	13.0	16.2	19.0
Meat and meat products	6.5	6.5	6.5	15.0	18.0	20.0
Salt (unpacked)	20.0	26.0	26.0	47.0	47.0	50.0
Cotton fabrics	3.0	5.5	7.7	5.5	9.2	12.0
Leather shoes	4.6	6.0	7.7	7.0	8.7	15.0
Knitted products	5.2	8.2	9.7	8.0	10.2	15.0
Fish and fish products	7.0	9.0	10.5	12.0	16.0	18.0
Clothing	5.8	6.7	9.2	8.0	11.2	15.0
Soap	5.5	7.2	7.2	7.2	10.2	25.0
Chinaware	12.0	15.0	15.0	16.0	22.0	35.0
Furniture	9.0	11.0	12.0	13.0	15.0	20.0

SOURCE: Gogol', 1958, p. 276, 1960, p. 390.

10 indicates there is no variation in the rebate on bread, Table 9 shows that the price varies.

The procedure for determining the margin for restaurants is somewhat more complicated. Like the retail stores, the restaurant is given a rebate on the cost of the food items it purchases. However, restaurants add a markup (*natsenka*) to the retail price to compensate for the cost of preparing the goods. As of 1956, there were three types of markups depending on the elegance of the restaurant (Lavrov, 1956, pp. 148–49). This procedure resembles more closely the Western practice of markup above cost than does the method of using a rebate.

Before the financial plan can be issued, the physical plan for retail sales must be drawn up. The composition of the items to be sold determines the total revenue and specific markup. If it should become necessary to alter the physical plan, the financial plan would also have to be changed. In drawing up the financial plan, therefore, the physical plan must be known in advance, as well as the wholesale price gross of the turnover tax, the retail price, and the rebate of the goods to be sold. After making an estimate of what the costs of distribution will be, planned profits can be derived by subtracting distribution costs from the rebate. The financial plan is thus concerned with the inflow of revenue to the retailer and the outflow of his payments to cover both the cost of his goods and the cost of distribution. The remaining figure in the financial plan is planned profit.

Not all retail outlets have financial plans. The smaller organizations do not operate on a *khozraschet* basis (independent financial accounting system), in which expenditures are to be covered by revenues obtained from the sale of goods and services. Accordingly, the financial transactions of the smaller organizations are often included in the financial plan of the superior administrative and operational organizations.

In addition, there may be an over-all plan for a given region encompassing the activities of the administrative organizations and the operational plans of the retailing and wholesaling *khozraschet* organizations. The higher administrative organizations also include the capital expenditure accounts in their financial plan. Table 11 shows the composite financial plan for the Ministry of Trade of the USSR for 1956.

By establishing certain financial targets in the financial plan, the marketing authorities in the Ministry of Trade are able to compare and contrast the past and present records of a firm with those of similar firms. One of the

Table 11—Earnings and Expenditure Flow for Trade Organizations in the Ministry of Trade USSR for 1956 (in Million Rubles)

Income

1. Profit		758.6
2. Amortization, including for		42.2
a. Capital investment	12.6	
b. Capital repair	29.7	
3. Miscellaneous		6.0
Total		806.8

Expenditures

1. Financing capital investment	38.2
2. Capital repair expenditures	29.7
3. Growth of own working capital	6.1
4. Deductions for director's fund	.5
5. Improvement of auxiliary operations	7.0
6. Income earned from agriculture to be distributed	4.2
7. Reducing loans for mechanical equipment	1.4
Total	87.0

Relation to State Budget

1. Allocated for capital investment in addition to amortization	5.7
2. Remainder (total profit — minus expenditures — addition to capital investment)	725.4

SOURCE: Gogol', 1958, p. 344.

most important methods for accomplishing this is the use of the profit and loss statement in the form of a financial plan. But officials of the Ministry of Trade are not the only ones in a position to exercise financial control; state banking and financial agencies also have considerable power.

CREDIT

Before discussing how the monetary and financial organizations use the financial plan and the anticipated inflow and outflow of funds for purposes of control, it is necessary to examine another aspect of the financial planning operation: the issuance of credit to trade organizations and its effect on both working and fixed capital. It is primarily through credit, an integral part of financial planning, that the state banking authorities are able to control and direct the development of trade and distribution.

An indication of the importance of the credit activities of Gosbank, the banking source of short-term credit, is that as of January, 1961, the amount of short-term money invested in trade agencies equaled 13.5 billion rubles (TsSU 5, p. 849). This is an increase over the 6 billion rubles of loans granted trade organizations by Gosbank as of January, 1956, and 8.8 billion rubles as of January, 1957. About one half of the short-term credit issued to trade organizations is allocated to consumer cooperatives. Since the consumer cooperatives have a lower volume of retail sales than government stores, this implies that cooperative dependence on Gosbank for credit is especially important. Moreover, approximately 70 per cent of all the short-term borrowed working capital is held in the form of inventory. All of this suggests the scale and significance of Gosbank's activities (Lisitsian, 1957, p. 26; Mezhiborskaia and Mosikovich, Jan., 1956, p. 27).

Distribution organizations in the Soviet Union require credit for much the same reason that such organizations all over the world need credit. When a retail or wholesale organization is opened, it is given an outright financial gift in the form of a bank account so that it may acquire a working inventory and make other financial expenditures prior to the sale of any goods. Traditionally, however, the Soviet firm's "own working capital" is less than is needed to satisfy their everyday inventory demands. Consequently, the enterprise, with the approval of its trade organization, applies to Gosbank for short-term credit loans primarily for inventory. A request and promise to pay *(zaiavlenie-obiazatel'stvo)* is made out and turned over to the bank. This is equivalent to our ninety-day self-liquidating commercial paper in that the loan is to be repaid with the proceeds of the sale of the goods financed by the use of the loan. This would be the procedure not only for normal inventory needs but also for the purchase of seasonal stocks and other temporary loans needed because of early shipment and other emergencies.

Occasionally it is also necessary for the enterprise to supplement its working capital for reasons not connected with commodity purchases. The store may be rearranging its layout or introducing some new service for which a short-term loan is required. In this case, a declaration *(zaiavlenie)* is made out, which the bank will accept or reject. If the loan is approved, then, as differentiated from the commodity loan procedure described above, an additional step is required in which a note *(srochnye obiazatel'stvo)* must be signed.

Short-term bank loans (a loan up to 12 months) are issued by Gosbank. Generally, interest is paid, and as of January 1, 1955, the maximum rate was 2 per cent, except for a 3 per cent rate charged on overdue loans. As of July 26, 1955, Gosbank could also issue loans up to two years in duration provided the funds were to be used for introducing technological improvements (Genkin and Fialkov, 1957, p. 181; Ushakov, 1956, p. 11).

Gosbank also disburses funds for capital repairs and capital construction if they are under 10,000 rubles. Capital repairs are almost solely taken from the firm's depreciation account. In 1957, out of a total of 55.7 million rubles deducted for depreciation, 30.5 million were set aside for capital repairs. The depreciation norm of a building is 4.3 per cent, of which 1.8 per cent is authorized for repairs and 2.5 per cent for capital construction or amortization. This is equivalent to the 4 per cent figure allowed by the New York Temporary Rent Control Commission, but the conditions of the buildings in the two countries somehow differ. For trade equipment, the depreciation rate is 7 per cent with 5.5 per cent designated for repairs and 1.5 per cent for capital reconstruction. The highest depreciation allowance is for outdoor stalls, which are depreciated at a rate of 20 per cent of total value annually (Makarov, 1956, pp. 83, 89; Birman, 1957, Vol. II, p. 264; Tsymbal, Oct., 1958, p. 49).

Because of their long-term nature, large capital expenditures are usually financed through a special bank. Until the mid-1950's, capital grants to trade organizations were all supervised by Torgbank, a bank created specially for this. Its successor, Stroibank, an all-purpose long-term credit bank, now allocates the long-term construction funds, which are derived from several sources. These funds are made up of deductions for depreciation and amortization, proceeds of a fund built up from 50 per cent of the organization's earnings after deduction of planned profits, and direct contributions from the government budget. On occasion, money is also added from the Director's Fund, which is made up of funds from both planned and unplanned profits. As of January 1, 1958, the capital assets of the distribution network were valued at 910 million rubles, evaluated at original cost (Tsymbal, Oct., 1958, p. 49; Ikonnikov, 1959, p. 37).

CONTROL THROUGH GOSBANK

While financial planning is necessary in any industrial society in which goods are produced in advance anticipation of sale, it is also used in the Soviet Union as a means of supervising the financial and, therefore, the operating activities of the various enterprises under state control. The financial plan is well suited for this purpose since it not only projects profit and loss, it also charts inflow and outflow of funds at the same time that it controls the issuance and repayment of debt. The total effect of these measures plus the collection of turnover taxes encompasses what the Soviets call "control by the ruble."

As mentioned before, financial control is exercised by both units of the Ministry of Trade and Gosbank. Since the control techniques in financial planning used by the Ministry of Trade resemble their physical planning procedures, a description of the methods used by the Ministry of Trade to supervise and regulate financial activity would be repetitive. To understand the novel aspects of financial credit in Russian marketing, the measures utilized by Gosbank and the other monetary agencies must be studied.

The significance of Gosbank's power over the distribution network becomes apparent when it is pointed out that cash transactions play a small role in the normal operation of the typical Soviet enterprise. Except for wage payments and limited cash purchases of agricultural products from the peasants, financial transactions are almost always conducted by means of an interchange through Gosbank. While the check system as it has developed in the United States is not common in the Soviet Union, much the same type of activity is carried out at the enterprise level through a system of clearing operations handled by the banks. In dealing with one another, firms expend and receive ruble credits within the confines of Gosbank. It is estimated that at least 90 per cent of Soviet monetary transactions are conducted not in cash but in such clearinghouse adjustments.* Gosbank therefore has continual and direct control over almost all major financial interfirm transactions. It is in a position to know what is being ordered from whom and from where and to evaluate whether or not this commercial activity of the trade enterprise is in keeping with the financial plan.

But Gosbank's power is not restricted to observing daily financial flows. As mentioned earlier, Russian trade organizations are normally forced to request short-term loans from Gosbank to supplement their "own working capital." Frequently it is also necessary to satisfy temporary needs with special seasonal loans. Consequently, through the issuance of credit, Gosbank is able to control the intended, as well as the actual, use of funds.

While control over the issuance of credit is an important prerogative, it is necessary to describe how a normal business transaction is conducted between Soviet

---

* This is actually not too surprising since it is estimated that almost 80 per cent of the commercial transactions in the United States are handled through checking accounts, which means within the walls of the banking system (Board of Governors of the Federal Reserve System, *Federal Reserve Bulletin,* Washington, Sept., 1961, p. 1057).

distribution enterprises in order to appreciate the full extent of Gosbank's control power. While the Russians are not as sophisticated in their business dealings as are American businessmen, there is none the less considerable variety in the manner in which they ship and purchase goods. To simplify the following explanation, only the most common commercial transactions and Gosbank control procedures will be described. (The main sources for the information about to be presented are Genkin and Fialkov, 1957, pp. 195 ff., and Makarov, 1955, pp. 150 ff., and Makarov, 1956, pp. 39 ff.)

The two major methods by which goods are exchanged between firms are the acceptance (*aktseptnaia*) and the accreditation (*akkreditivnaia*) systems. The more common of the two, the acceptance method, is equivalent to payment by draft, while the accreditation method resembles a letter of credit.

With the acceptance system, two major documents are required, the invoice (*schet-faktura*) and the draft (*plate-zhnoe trebovanie*). As the product leaves the supplier, it is accompanied by the invoice, which simply catalogs the shipment. Simultaneously, a copy of the invoice and the necessary transportation documents are attached to the draft and sent to the supplier's bank. The supplier's bank, in turn, dispatches the document to the buyer's bank. This is called the acceptance (*aktseptnaia*) method because the out-of-town buyer has three working days to accept or reject the shipment after notification arrives from the bank that it has received the draft. If the buyer accepts, he notifies his bank, which transfers money from his account to the supplier's bank, which then transfers it to the supplier's account.

The accreditation (*akkreditivnaia*) method is used

when the transaction is an unusual one, when no formal relations exist between the buyer and the seller, or when the buyer's credit is weak. In such cases, the buyer is the first one to contact his bank. He asks that a letter of credit (*akkreditivnoe poruchenie*) be sent to the supplier's bank. After the supplier is informed that sufficient funds exist, he ships the goods and notifies his bank. His bank then contacts the buyer's bank, and the funds are immediately transferred to the supplier's account. Only after the funds have been reassigned does the supplier's bank send the invoice and other documents to the buyer's bank in order that they may be passed on to the buyer.

As mentioned earlier, cash is rarely used in such transactions. Normally a cash purchase may be made without the permission of Gosbank only if the amount does not exceed 50 rubles. Some firms also have the use of checks, either from a special account or from a special checkbook with a limited number of checks and with the maximum amount for which the checks may be written prescribed in advance.

Before leaving the discussion of the commercial transaction process, it should be noted that special clearinghouses have been created to expedite the clearing process, especially between organizations having many reciprocal ties. The BVR (Biuro Vzaimnyky Raschetov), or Bureau for Reciprocal Accounting, operates as a unit of Gosbank and, by balancing together various interdependent accounts, is able to simplify the bookkeeping work involved.

The reasons that a distributor needs working capital should be clear by now. He must have funds at his disposal so that the supplies he has ordered can be purchased. Moreover, he must also have funds available to pay the employees who have first claim to all funds. As the retailer sells his purchases, his financial standing is restored and he is able to pay back loans and buy more goods. It is at this stage that the control activities of Gosbank are needed to insure that the funds are directed in an approved and constructive fashion.

When Gosbank issues credit to a retail enterprise, a special account is opened if it is intended that the funds will be used to purchase inventory. At least a portion of the firm's own working capital is also held there. This special loan account (*spetsial'nnyi ssudnyi schet*) is tapped every time it is necessary to pay a supplier's draft. The remainder of the firm's funds are held in a regular transactions account (*raschetnyi schet*), which is used to pay other expenses such as wages and utility bills.

When the goods are sold by the retailer, the proceeds are used to replenish the two accounts. The sales receipts first flow into the special loan account, where they are used to pay off the bank loan and replenish the firm's own working capital. Then every five days the rebate (*skidka*) from the sales price is transferred from the special loan account to the transaction account, which is then used to finance the various costs of distribution. The transaction account is also normally used to make all payments to the government in the form of profits tax.

On the wholesale level, another account plays an important role. As sales receipts are turned over to the wholesaler, turnover tax payments are transferred directly from the special loan account to the account of the Ministry of Finance. While the frequency with which the transfers are made depends on the sales volume of the commodities involved, the flow of such taxes provides another lever of financial control.

With such powers, Gosbank and the Ministry of Finance are in unique positions both to control the nature of economic activity and to guide the operations of the trade organizations. The ability to lend more to those projects the state desires to encourage is a basic instrument in determining the very character of the national economy. Similarly, by comparing actual financial developments specified in the plan or recorded in the past, banking officials are normally able to pinpoint any operational shortcomings. Control of the purse has always been a powerful weapon, and while it is occasionally abused, it is not only a method for insuring that the interests of the state are being effectively and honestly served but also is a means by which constructive advice may be offered.

Moreover, because of the monopolistic nature of the bank, it is possible to supervise and keep abreast of both local market conditions and the state of marketing and sales throughout the whole country. The problem of assembling statistical data from independently owned organizations does not exist. National financial and sales indices of the Soviet Union are already in the hands of a single entity. Once the data are consolidated, appropriate steps can be taken immediately.

LOOPHOLES IN CONTROL

With all these powers, Gosbank is normally able to ascertain and influence the efficiency of the whole distribution sector. There are several factors, however, that complicate the procedure. First, there is a mechanical problem connected with the application of the rebate (*skidka*).

Second, Gosbank is not the sole source of credit for trade organizations. In some cases, the percentage of "own working capital" out of the total may be unduly increased so that, in effect, Gosbank credit is used only for a fraction of the total expenditures. In other instances, because merchandise is shipped before payment is collected, the supplier may bear an excessive share of the working capital credit. Third, the practice of completing the bulk of the plan only in the last days of the planning period tends to bunch the need for commercial credit into certain segments of the period instead of smoothing out the need over even intervals. As each factor is examined in detail, it will be seen that sometimes the repayment of a Gosbank loan may not necessarily be an indication of the over-all financial progress of the retail firm.

As shown in Table 10, the rebate varies with each type of product. This means that theoretically it is necessary to know what the particular rebate is on each product. However, to simplify the construction of the original financial plan, an average rate of rebate is utilized. Thus, the actual pattern of sales may be such that the rebate collected diverges from the average planned rate. The result may be that the firm has more, or fewer, funds at its disposal than originally intended in the financial plan. Varying rates of rebate also pose a bookkeeping problem for Gosbank, which must know the particular rebate on each type of goods. The more the rate varies, the more difficult it is for the bank to determine the proper allocation of credits (Davydov and Kuprienko, July, 1961, p. 27; Genkin and Fialkov, 1957, p. 183).

Gosbank is only one of the three normal sources of credit. In addition to the initial grant of "own working capital" granted to all new firms, credit is also obtained from suppliers in the form of accounts payable. (See Figure 6.) In the 1930's, "own working capital" accounted for only 30 per cent of the total inventory needs of the trade network. This involved Gosbank in almost all normal activities and led to undue participation in even routine distribution activities, from which Gosbank should have been excluded. As part of the general reaction that followed Stalin's death, it was decided to give trade enterprises more freedom. Consquently the share of "own working capital" was increased to 60 per cent, and the share of bank credit was lowered from 60 per cent to 20 per cent (Lisitsian, 1957, pp. 37-38). It was immediately discovered that in some instances Gosbank lost almost all of its control. As a result, in September, 1955, Gosbank issued a new decree allowing the firm to own 50 per cent of its credit and increased the bank's share to 30 per cent, a move of

Figure 6—Sources of Short-term Credit and Their Applications

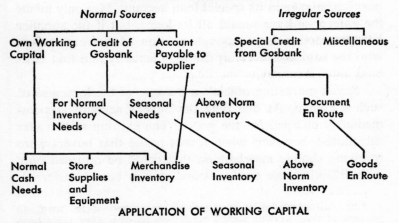

SOURCES OF WORKING CAPITAL

SOURCE: Makarov, 1956, p. 52.

10 per cent in each direction (Lisitsian, 1957, p. 40; Birman, 1957, p. 259).*

Gosbank and "own" funds usually account for approximately 80 per cent of the retailer's working capital. The remaining unaccounted-for portion of short-term credit is provided to the firm by its suppliers. While this amounted to only 17 per cent in 1956, at times it does become larger and in 1952 amounted to 25 per cent of the total (Lisitsian, 1957, pp. 36, 42, 44). To a large extent, the credit provided by the supplier arises because of the delay in processing the papers accompanying the transaction. Lisitsian complains that it normally takes ten days for the documents to make the circuit and for the buyer's bank account to be affected. It is possible, therefore, that goods ordered and delivered immediately thereafter may be sold before the supplier is paid. This could mean that the buyer need have no recourse to bank credit at all; and, in effect, he may even use the supplier's funds to make additional purchases. It is even possible that an enterprise may find itself with a positive balance in its special loan account. Not only might the enterprise have repaid all its loans, but if the supplier has provided a large enough portion of the enterprise's working capital, the enterprise may actually find that Gosbank owes it money.

Soviet marketing officials are aware of the looseness of such a system. At one time the buyer's account was immediately charged for the goods. The existing system was substituted, however, when it was found that buyers were receiving shoddy merchandise that could be returned only with difficulty once the funds had already been transferred.

---

* Specialized wholesale organizations are authorized to "own" 40 per cent of their working capital needs because of a more rapid turnover, while consumer cooperatives are allowed only 15 per cent.

While they may desire to speed up the bookkeeping process, they realize that as long as the *aktseptnaia* method is used and the buyer is given an opportunity to reject the goods, some delay is inevitable (Spasskii, "Nuzhen li Predvaritel'nyi Aktsept?" *Den'gi i Kredit,* Dec., 1956, p. 29; Lisitsian, 1957, p. 110).

The effectiveness of using the credit position of the enterprise as a gauge of operating efficiency is further affected by the phenomenon known as storming (*shturmovshchina*). Despite (or because of) the planned nature of the Soviet economy, there is a tendency for all organizations to concentrate their activities in the last portion of any planning period. This practice creates serious problems throughout the rest of the economy and also affects the financial operations of the distribution network. During the last portion of the planning period, the supplier ships the bulk of his goods, and the buyer may receive 50–55 per cent of his total month's supply in this period. Since the goods are not immediately sold to the consumer, the demand for and use of credit increases. Thus, the retail firm may find itself overdrawn on credit at the same time it is meeting, or even overfulfilling, its trade plan.

Consequently, if the bank's role in supplying credit is unduly reduced or if uneven shipments and credit needs occur, the credit position of a trade enterprise may not be an accurate measure of operational efficiency. Not only may this invalidate the significance of the firm's credit position as an indicator of successful management, it may also reduce the effectiveness of Gosbank's credit control.

It sometimes happens, of course, that despite the competence of Gosbank's controls, other difficulties develop. Because the planned profit figure is a residue, it is possible for an enterprise to operate at a net loss. This may be the result of extravagance, poor management, or a faulty physical plan.* In early 1954, there were 2,253 unprofitable (*ubytochnye*) firms. The number had apparently been reduced somewhat by 1956, although in 1958, 3–4 per cent of all retail firms were reported to have lost money (Tiukov, May, 1954, p. 3; *Sovetskaia Torgovlia,* May 22, 1956, p. 3, July, 1961, p. 26; Gogol', 1958, p. 326).

If a firm begins to operate in the red, it is likely to find it difficult to pay back its loans when they are due. In such an event, Gosbank will begin to exercise closer control. Receipts are set aside for the purpose of paying off specific debts, and notice is given to the superior administrative organization of the enterprise. The responsible administration may then choose to guarantee the debts of its subordinate unit if it appears that the financial difficulty is only temporary. In any case, both administrative and financial controls are tightened.

For firms that have had no trouble until this point, help is readily made available. For the others, their suppliers are notified and warned to demand either letters of credit or some other form of payment in advance. Furthermore, the firm in financial trouble is restricted in its use of special loan accounts (*spetsial'nnyi ssudnyi schet*), and almost all its transactions must be paid from the transaction account (*raschetnyi schet*). If after six months, there is no reduction in the size of losses, no increase in working capital, and no payment of old debts, the bank is empowered to

---

* When it is the last, inflationary pressures are often created. If the batch of goods prescribed in the original plan cannot be sold, this may make it difficult to collect turnover taxes and other anticipated budget revenues. Since income has been paid to the producing factors but not reabsorbed by the state, it is possible that an inflationary gap will be created, especially if it is necessary to issue more credit in order to produce and stock goods that will sell (Lisitsian, 1957, p. 93).

declare the firm bankrupt *(neplatezhesposobnyi)*. Fifteen days after the superior trade organization has been notified of this proposed action, Gosbank publishes the official declaration in a specially issued bulletin (Ushakov, 1956, p. 51).

Once the official notice has been published, a special commission is established to review and revamp the operation of the bankrupt firm. While the composition of such commissions has changed from time to time, it is usually made up of representatives of the Ministry of Government Control, Gosbank, the Ministry of Finance, and the Ministry of Trade. This special commission has the power to suspend all credit grants and order the sale of existing stocks to other organizations. Consequently, while financial control in the Soviet Union usually implies supervision over operating enterprises, if need be it may also involve the unpleasant task of liquidation.

CONCLUSION

In conclusion, the financial plan encompassing over-all performance and the allocation of credit is an important and, generally, an effective instrument of control in trade and distribution. Such control is necessary in all societies. It is essential to have some measure for evaluating the proper performance of marketing tasks, especially those involving the use of financial resources. Moreover, if someone is to offer his funds so that the gap caused by production in advance of ultimate sale can be breeched, the lender must have some protection. The financial plan is one means of safeguarding these financial resources. For interested

organizations, especially the Ministry of Trade and Gosbank, the financial plan provides an opportunity to inspect
and supervise the operation of marketing enterprises.

While, for the most part, Soviet financial control is
effective, occasionally there may be some difficulty. Because
credit is obtainable from sources other than Gosbank, it is
possible that Gosbank may not be completely aware of all
the activities of an enterprise. Furthermore, to the extent
that the physical plan is faulty, the financial plan will be
defective. This may involve reworking the financial plan
so that it corresponds to the revised physical plan. On
occasion it may involve bankruptcy. As will be seen in the
next chapter, the use of two plans may also require that
they be adjusted to one another in order to obtain con-
sistency and to prevent conflict, which otherwise might
create unintended results. Within these limitations, however, financial control is a powerful weapon and an important adjunct to other types of planning in Soviet distribution.

[6] *THE HUMAN ELEMENT AND STATE OWNERSHIP*

INTRODUCTION

TO ANYONE who has ever worked in a large bureaucratic organization, the problems of accountability, honesty, and incentive are very familiar. This is the case whether the organization be a governmental unit like the United States Army, an educational institution like Harvard University, or a commercial organization like the Chrysler Corporation. As an organization grows in size, it becomes necessary to delegate authority. Once this is done, it is equally imperative to institute controls. There must be some assurance that work is proceeding in the best interests of the absentee owners and that no one is abusing the trust and power delegated to him. If only preventive checks were needed, however, the problem would not be especially complicated. But since development and future growth is usually the *raison d'être* for the organization, it is also necessary to

129

provide some positive stimulus in the form of incentives. The difficulty arises, therefore, when the restraints begin to inhibit creativity or, conversely, when freedom of action becomes so unrestrained that the best interests of the absentee owners are placed in jeopardy.

Although frequently the main issues, checks on honesty together with incentives for creativity are not the only problems involved in such a system. Standards of performance and measures of relative efficiency are also needed to assure those not on the scene that the honest men are doing a capable job. It is not enough to say that nothing has been stolen or that the firm did not operate at a loss; it is also necessary to demonstrate how the organization performed relative to other organizations or to some absolute standard.

Safeguarding the interests of absentee owners is not a new problem. The concept of the absentee landlord is as old as ancient history. With the onset of the industrial revolution, however, absentee ownership took on a new dimension as manufacturing enterprises grew in size. As organizations became larger and more diverse, the problems of checks, incentives, and standards became more complicated. Moreover, manufactured products and equipment were usually more valuable than similar items in agriculture. Consequently, greater trust and more elaborate forms of supervision were placed on those to whom authority was delegated. The problem became even more complex as owners absented themselves from the active supervision of the distribution functions, for here there was cause for concern not just because the assets were valuable, but also because they were portable and therefore more easily stolen.

DELEGATED AUTHORITY
IN THE SOVIET UNION
AND ITS CONSEQUENCES

Because almost all industrial and commercial property is owned by the state, the Soviet Union represents an interesting case study of how absentee ownership affects the service and efficiency of operations in the distribution of consumers' goods. In a system where almost all responsibility and authority is delegated, certain problems have developed that are different from those operative in a system where the owner is also the working manager. This chapter will discuss some of the difficulties confronted by the Russians and how they attempt to offset them through both negative and positive means—controls and incentives. It should be noted that such problems are not necessarily confined to a society in which the state owns the means of production and distribution. These conditions may also exist in the capitalistic system when the owner delegates operational responsibility to a manager.

The Need for Security

In the Soviet distribution process, it is necessary to entrust individuals with state-owned assets, both fixed (factories, stores, and fixtures) and current (merchandise and money). As a means of protecting the interests of the absentee owner (the Council of Ministers or the Presidium of the Communist Party), the individual is usually made accountable for the state property under his control. The Russians have institutionalized this process, calling it "material responsibility." In other words, if goods are stolen or damaged, the responsible official is personally liable.* As mentioned before, this is necessary in a large organization because the absentee owner insists on some control over the property being used. Because he is not present himself, the owner attempts by this means to create the feeling of personal ownership and responsibility in the subordinate official with the hope that the agent or employee will then act as the owner would himself.

Operating under such a system, the Russian store official, who is materially responsible, is likely to insist on very rigid controls in the storing and selling of goods. Of necessity, he must often entrust "his" merchandise to others until the goods are turned over to the consumer. To insure that he, too, is fully protected, the official with material responsibility uses as many control procedures and double-checking devices as possible. He must make certain that his subordinates are carefully regulated and do not steal at his, or the state's expense. In fact, the official who is materially responsible may be more concerned about preserving the goods than about carrying out his basic operational tasks. To this individual, prevention of theft is often more important than facilitation of sales.

The adaptation of the cashier (kassa) system is an example of how the use of precautionary measures has affected service. In order to insure maximum security, under the cashier system the unattended customer is not allowed to examine any commodity, the salesclerk is not

---

* When discussing such problems, one finds many analogies in the U.S. Army. When an army officer "signs out" for the property in his unit, he is responsible for all losses.

allowed to take cash, and the cashier is not allowed to handle any goods. As described in Chapter 2, when the customer enters the store, he must approach the salesclerk at the counter and ask the price. If the customer desires to examine the merchandise, the salesclerk must be asked to pass the items over the counter. Having ascertained the price and having returned the goods, the customer must move to the cashier's booth, pay the ruble value of the goods, and obtain a receipt. It is then necessary to return to the salesclerk and turn over the receipt before the goods will be transferred. This usually necessitates standing in at least three lines for each type of product purchased.

It seems clear that one of the important explanations for the tenacity and ubiquity of this cumbersome system in the Soviet Union is the material responsibility that is placed on the management of the store. The cashier system permits double and even triple checking of goods and cash receipts. The cashier's receipts can be independently calculated against the salesclerk's records to insure that the proper cash amount has been collected. The salesclerk's inventory, in turn, can be checked against receipts. Such a system also reduces the danger of shoplifting. In a self-service operation, on the other hand, the degree of control is lessened considerably. Anyone, clerk or customer, may handle the goods, and consequently anyone may pocket them. Naturally, this has been an impediment to the introduction of self-service and the greater convenience it brings.

The same situation effects the operation of Russian restaurants. To insure that the waiters will not steal food, it is normal procedure to require each waiter to pay for every item he takes from the kitchen as he orders it. This means the waiter must wait in several lines merely to obtain the food for one table. While it is true that this reduces dishonesty, it also means that restaurant service is generally very poor. It also means that the waiter is contantly handling money *and* food, which is not particularly hygienic.

Control through Goal Fulfillment

A second major instrument of control that has been evolved in the Soviet Union to cope with the problem of delegated authority is a system of performance or work criteria. Since it is no longer possible for the owner himself on the basis of personal contact to judge performance and the effectiveness of the firm's operations, certain impersonal procedures are required.* For the absentee owner in the Soviet Union, some common denominator is needed to compare efficiency of performance among the various related and unrelated sectors of the economy.

Such judgments are usually based on the fulfillment of certain preconceived goals. Since almost everyone—from the salesclerk to the Minister of Trade—is striving to meet his particular goal, it is often possible to make interpersonal or interunit comparisons of ability by measuring the degree of goal fulfillment or overfulfillment. As long as the work being performed can be expressed in measurable goals, this is usually a workable system. Unfortunately, not all goals, especially those affecting quality and service, are measurable. Moreover, because there are so many organizations that must be regulated in the Soviet Union, performance goals and maintenance procedures are usually standardized. Of necessity, the specialized nature of a par-

---

* In the U.S. Army, subordinate officials are often judged by their superiors, who must make out character or efficiency reports.

ticular operation is merged with the problems of the many. A frequent result, as will be shown below, is that there is an accommodation to the prescribed standard, often at the expense of other more desirable objectives.

While questions of industrial production have generally been outside the scope of this study, it is necessary here to consider certain practices that have an important effect on the conduct of trade and distribution. These difficulties arise because for the most part, industrial managers in the Soviet Union are not concerned about winning and holding wholesale and retail buyers. As mentioned earlier, the most important task of managers in the state-owned society of the Soviet Union is to fulfill certain preassigned goals. To eliminate excessive detail, the industrial goals are usually specified in such general forms as gross ruble value of production and/or physical quantity (number of items or weight). The manager is more concerned about fulfilling these goals than about making a profit.

This practice in industry affects distribution when the trade officials approach the factory and try to purchase goods for their customers. In the late 1950's, store managers began to report with increasing frequency that factories were refusing to produce the particular models or assortments of goods desired by the store managers. Since the factory manager is responsible only for the success indicators that are established for the industry as a whole, he often finds that he must ignore the requests of the store manager if he is to fulfill his plan.

Illustrations of how the store manager is affected when factory managers are concerned only about meeting their production targets have been given by M. Bespalov, the assistant director of Soiuzglavtorg under Gosplan, the Office for Interrepublic Distribution of Consumers' Goods

(*Sovetskaia Torgovlia,* Aug. 20, 1960, p. 3; *Pravda,* Apr. 8, 1960, p. 2). On the one hand, the establishment of the production goals in terms of gross rubles may cause dissatisfaction. Bespalov cites a situation in which the store managers wanted the factories to produce a cheap fabric. The manufacturers refused because production of the cheaper goods would have made it harder for them to meet their production goal, which was in terms of gross ruble output. On the other hand, when the production goal is projected in terms of physical weight, there may also be trouble. For example, the success of enamelware production is judged by fulfillment of plan goals that are established in tons. The result is that manufacturers tend to favor large heavy pieces and neglect the production of the more frequently demanded smaller enamelware.

Yet if both monetary and quantitative criteria are used together, the store managers may still find their needs neglected. Watch and camera production goals are established in terms of both units of output and value of production. This means that if store managers should desire a high-priced assortment of these items, factory managers may be unwilling to produce them because this might affect their success in fulfilling the quantitative portion of their goal.

Such situations are not without remedy. The goals of the production plan can be altered and usually are when these difficulties are brought to light. However, inflexibilities of this nature are likely to arise when absentee ownership necessitates the formation of general goals for the purpose of solving complex and specific issues. Moreover, since there is one set of goals for the production sector and another set for the distribution sector, a mismatching of aims is possible. As consumer demand in the Soviet

Union becomes more difficult to satisfy (see Chapter 3), there is increased likelihood of such divergence.

Not only does confusion arise because production and trade officials adhere to two different sets of goals, the use of goals in the marketing sector creates a problem in itself. What kind of goals can the absentee owner establish in trade? In the Soviet Union, they use sales volume expressed in rubles. Since trade, like production, is multidimensional, this is frequently inadequate. When undue emphasis is placed on a narrow aspect of the whole economic process, undesired effects are often created. For example, from the consumer's point of view it is not only necessary to have available the proper assortment and quality of goods, it is also necessary to provide that intangible known as service. Unfortunately, it is difficult to measure service in quantitative terms. As a result, it is all but impossible to include service goals as targets that must be met in the over-all fulfillment of the plan.

The tendency, then, is for the store manager to neglect service for the more important task of sales volume upon which his record is based. Normally, of course, the volume of sales depends on the consumers' satisfaction with a store's service. In the Soviet Union, however, the size of the trade network is woefully inadequate for the volume of goods being sold (*Sovetskaia Torgovlia,* June 2, 1960, p. 2; July 9, 1960, p. 1; Aug. 9, 1960, p. 1; Aug. 11, 1960, p. 1). Consequently, sales are more a function of the availability of sales outlets than the service of a particular store. While there are exceptions, there is thus little incentive within or without the plan for the store manager to improve service. Since service is such an important aspect of the complete distribution process, any tendency to neglect it can only negatively affect the operation of the marketing network from the point of view of the consumer.

While the major goal of marketing personnel is to sell the assigned ruble quota of goods, complications sometimes result because it is also necessary to make a profit in the process. It will be remembered that because of certain anomalies in the price and markup system, different types of goods entitle the manager to different rebate allowances *(skidki)*. Therefore, it is sometimes possible for the store manager to select his assortment of goods in such a way that he manages a little extra profit. Unfortunately, the most profitable assortment for the manager does not always mean the most satisfactory selection of goods for the consumer. For example, the store may offer a more expensive frying pan because it means a higher rebate, whereas the consumer may actually prefer a cheaper model.

Because of the profit motive, the system of rebate allowances may also cause trouble at the wholesale level. Complaints have been published about certain wholesale organizations that unnecessarily ship goods to intermediate wholesale bases under their jurisdiction in order to collect an extra rebate. (The proper procedure would have been to send the goods directly to the retailer.) To enlist the retailer's help in preventing such waste, the state has authorized retailers to keep the whole rebate if the goods are sent directly from factory to retailer. The inevitable result is frequent friction between retailers and wholesalers.

There is one further example illustrating the problems that arise in marketing because generalized goals are postulated for specific situations. It is acknowledged that a certain amount of normal waste and damage will occur in the process of moving and storing goods on their way from the factory to the consumer. A specified percentage of the sales volume, therefore, is allocated in advance to cover this normal loss. Because this norm is assigned in a blanket fashion over large areas, it frequently happens that a store may have less spoilage than it was authorized. The rules state that if this happens, the manager is supposed to report it to his supervisory organization and turn back the already allocated goods. Apparently many Soviet managers have realized the potentialities of such a system. This is well illustrated in a *Krokodil* cartoon. An assistant in a shop is shown explaining to a customer that the manager is taking inventory of the shrinkage loss norms. In the back of the store, the manager is seen around a fully laden dinner table with his friends, all of whom are busy devouring the "normed waste" (*Krokodil,* No. 33, 1957, p. 5). Distortions like this appear to be an inevitable result of reducing all standards to a common denominator.

Controls through Bureaucracy

The need to safeguard property and establish plan targets implies that lines of control and communication exist between the absentee owner and the operational units. If authority is to be delegated, there must be some instrument available for the transmission of instructions from the chief agent of the absentee owners. It cannot be assumed that the materially responsible official at the local level will necessarily perform his duty voluntarily. The reports of plan fulfillment must be checked, verified, and processed. Furthermore, if the enterprises being controlled are scattered and numerous enough, some means must be provided for on-the-spot inspections and transmission and consolidation of reports. Failure to do so will make it impossible for the ultimate authorities at the peak of the administrative pyramid to digest the findings and still have time to control the whole operation. Inevitably, bureaucracy is the result.

Many of the acts of the bureaucracy are beneficial and positive, especially in the early stages of its existence, when it makes decisions and acts primarily as an agent for the absentee owner. However, as the size of the administrative unit and the scope of its activities expand, the system of bureaucracy often takes on a dynamic life of its own. It sometimes happens that a bureaucratic staff will continue to grow despite the fact that its functions have diminished in importance. Moreover, what was once the means may become the end. As one sociologist has described the phenomena:

> Adherence to the rule, originally conceived as a means, becomes transformed into an end-in-itself; there occurs the familiar process of displacement of goals whereby an instrumental value becomes a terminal value.
>
> This emphasis, resulting from the displacement of the original goals, develops into rigidities and an inability to adjust readily. Formalism, even ritualism, ensues with an unchallenged insistence upon punctilious adherence to formalized procedures. This may be exaggerated to the point where primary concern with conformity to the rules interferes with the achievement of the purposes of the organization, in which case we have the familiar phenomenon of the technicism or red tape of the official (Merton, 1951, p. 155).*

As one of the largest marketing organizations in the world, the administrative apparatus of the Soviet distribution network closely fits the general pattern of bureaucratic

---

* For a humorous approach to the problem, see Parkinson (1957).

development. Its purpose is to protect the interests of the absentee owner—in this case, the state, as represented by the Council of Ministers of the USSR. Many of the activities of the Ministry of Trade are positive and are not necessarily related to the preservation of property or the enforcement of goal fulfillment. As described earlier, the Ministry of Trade and its organs introduce new forms of trade and help establish sales goals, prices, and general organizational structure of trade. Despite these positive contributions, however, certain problems are created as the Ministry of Trade and its bureaucracy grow in size and age, and this inevitably affects the efficiency of Soviet trade.

Both in scale and in function, the Ministry of Trade has a tendency to grow, and not always in directions that benefit the consumer. To the extent that excessive regulation and meaningless reports are required, costs are increased and service affected. The scale of bureaucratic activity can be judged from the number of reports that must be prepared. In the course of a year, the Ministry of Trade of the RSFSR alone sent out more than 260,000 papers, or the equivalent of 700 pounds of paper work a month (Nefedov, July, 1958, p. 25).* That such forms are often not essential is indicated by reports describing the curtailment of many such activities. From 1954 to 1956, 141 forms and reports were eliminated. This apparently pared the number of statistical indices and comparisons required of the bureaucracy from 639 to 69 a month, from 2,120 to 1,393 a quarter, and from 5,433 to 2,527 a year (Khrekin and Smoktii, May, 1956, p. 10; Gogol', 1957, p. 39).

---

* Undoubtedly, a special administrative unit was established to compile this information.

Perennially the Russians attempt to control their bureaucratic excesses. In the traditional manner, however, reducing the amount of work to be performed does not always mean that the administrative staff will be reduced. Anyone who has served in a bureaucratic organization can appreciate the predicament of the Ministry of Trade officials in the Moldavian Republic. After reorganizing their administrative staffs in both the government and cooperative networks to eliminate work duplication, it was found that the staffs were larger than before (*Sovetskaia Moldavia,* Nov. 29, 1957, p. 3; Jan. 5, 1958, p. 2).

Ironically enough, because of the rigidities engendered by the bureaucracy, it is sometimes necessary to pursue extralegal methods to achieve the original ends for which the bureaucracy was first created. As the procedures and rules become institutionalized, it becomes difficult to cope with unforeseen developments. Because supplies in the Soviet system are tightly controlled, formalized and complicated measures must be undertaken before any deviation from preplanned procedure is authorized. To provide flexibility, Soviet managers occasionally seek help from people called *tolkachi,* who have the proper connections. Their functions are the same as the expediters or gray-market operators that we periodically see in the West.

While the government is aware of the existence of such unauthorized activities, no all-out effort is made to stop them. Besides serving their own interests, *tolkachi* also serve the state by providing a certain flexibility in the operations of the economy. While *tolkachi* are frequently criticized and sometimes penalized, they are not normally placed in the same category as the outright criminals who sometimes manage their way into the bureaucracy and help only themselves (*Kommunist,* Jan. 10, 1958, p. 2; *Kommunist Tadzhikistana,* Feb. 28, 1958, p. 3).

Consequently, absentee ownership frequently involves the creation of certain institutions that affect the efficiency of operations. On the one hand, there is bred an atmosphere of caution and formality, while, on the other hand, there is a perversion of certain original goals. None the less, it is apparent that despite these difficulties the Soviet marketing system manages to move forward. Although material responsibility, goal fulfillment, and bureaucratic control may tend to inhibit creativity, there are other forces at work that stimulate it. Primarily, these are generated through the use of incentives and the introduction of improved work habits made possible by an improvement in the standard of living.

SOME POSITIVE FORCES

Incentives

The most potent force in the promotion of efficiency and growth in the Soviet Union is the carefully designed system of incentives. In the trade network, as in the other sectors of the economy, there are both material and psychological incentives.

Material incentives in the form of wages are generally regarded by the Russians as the most important stimuli. The wages of most managers and employees are dependent on the degree of plan fulfillment. While 90 per cent of the base wage is guaranteed as a minimum payment regardless of plan fulfillment, the worker's salary is increased proportionally as the plan is completed. For meeting the plan, a premium of 10 per cent is frequently paid. As the margin of plan overfulfillment increases, wages increase at an even faster rate. While not all pay schedules are the same, a typical example of the salary schedule is the one followed by the department store Dom Leningradskaia Torgovlia (House of Leningrad Trade) in Leningrad. The employees receive 120 per cent of their salary if the store plan is fulfilled by 105.1–110.0 per cent, and 130 per cent of their salary if the plan is overfulfilled by 110.1 to 115.0 per cent. This increase continues until salaries reach 170 per cent of the base amount.

Wages are also structured so that advanced educational training is encouraged. A premium is paid for those who have completed a formal course at one of the several trade institutes or one of the more numerous vocational training schools. Credit is also given for correspondence work relating to one's profession. Finally, employee suggestions that result in money-saving innovations are also encouraged by monetary rewards.

With salaries based on such incentives, managers and sales personnel generally feel a strong desire to fulfill the goals assigned to them. For the most part, this is an effective system. Nevertheless, some abuses occur. The difficulties that do result are usually a reflection of the pressure the individual feels to meet his goal. As was shown earlier, if the goal is unsuitably stated, something other than what was originally intended may be produced. Furthermore, the wage bonus may be so tempting that trade employees may sometimes artificially manipulate sales records to qualify for their bonuses. For instance, by means of uneven performance in the fulfillment of their monthly plan, TsUM Department Store in 1952 managed to obtain an undeserved 90 per cent wage premium. The store underfulfilled the plan by a substantial amount in the initial period, but the workers none the less received 90 per cent of their base pay. By overfulfilling the plan at the end of the period, progressive bonuses were paid, which more than compensated for the lost wages of the earlier period (Gatovskii, 1957, p. 200).

While monetary rewards are considered to provide the main stimulus, they are well supplemented with psychological incentives. The Russians are quite skilled in the use of this technique. Awards begin at the individual level. The title, Master (*otlichnik*) of Soviet Trade or Master of Soviet Cooking is presented to deserving sales and kitchen personnel. As of mid-1958, 37,000 people had been presented with such honors by the Ministry of Trade. The store itself may be presented with the "Red Banner." Such awards are similarly made to outstanding *oblast* organizations *(Sovetskaia Torgovlia,* Feb. 25, 1961, p. 3).* (This is reminiscent of the Army-Navy "E" that was awarded in the United States during World War II and that has been resurrected for firms that promote American exports.)

Appeals are also made to the pride of the employee. Trademarks are used. The worker is urged to make his firm's name and its symbol the most respected in the Soviet Union. The larger department stores each have their own symbol, which is displayed with the intention of creating a certain *esprit de corps.* This atmosphere is extended from

---

* There even seems to be a return to the glorification of the shock-worker, *udarnik,* in trade *(Sovetskaia Torgovlia,* Oct. 17, 1959, p. 1; Nov. 24, 1959, p. 1; Dec. 3, 1959, p. 1; May 31, 1960, p. 1).

the store level to the city level. Leningrad and Moscow compete with one another to offer the most "cultured" service and the best store operation.

Occasionally such appeals are even extended to the country as a whole. For example, Russian salesclerks have been told that "since the United States has been discredited by the U-2 incident, the whole world looks to the Soviet Union to set standards of honesty. Therefore it is now more important than ever that Soviet salesclerks conduct their sections honestly and properly" *(Sovetskaia Torgovlia,* June 4, 1960, p. 2).*

Improvement in the Standard of Living

Of the measures adopted by the Russians, the system of incentives seems the best-suited for dealing with the built-in hazards of delegated authority and absentee ownership. Recently, however, there have been indications that the excessive control and overregulation, as well as the overorganization, of the bureaucracy are being offset by other factors. As the standard of living in the Soviet Union improves and the conditions of scarcity are alleviated, there is likely to be somewhat less concern over the problem of honesty and the preservation of state property. As more trust is placed in the individual, he bears less watching. This has already taken the form of conductorless trolley buses in Moscow and several other large cities. In 1959–60, conductors were removed from many public transportation vehicles. The passenger now pays his fare voluntarily

---

* In this vein, Alexander Gerschenkron has suggested that one of the main functions of communist ideology is to provide a mass stimulus to workers in a country that is undergoing industrialization at a relatively late date ("Reflections on the Concept of Prerequisites of Modern Industrialization," *L'Industria,* No. 2, 1957, p. 16).

—without official supervision. The principle reportedly has even been extended to certain rural kiosks in the Ukraine where basic goods like sugar, salt, and soap are sold on an open table without the presence of a salesclerk.

It is not to be implied that preservation of state property is no longer a major issue. One reason the introduction of self-service has lagged in the Soviet Union is that individuals have been reluctant to assume material responsibility in a store with open shelves. A partial solution to the problem seems to be the use of joint material responsibility. Instead of one individual assuming responsibility, a group of three to five people in a working brigade collectively accept material responsibility. Such a system has only become feasible as material conditions have improved and as shoplifting has become somewhat less of a problem. None the less, material conditions have not improved that much, nor is dishonesty removed solely by an improvement in the standard of living. As a result, there is still considerable reluctance on the part of some employees to submit themselves to the risk of brigade material responsibility (*Sovetskaia Torgovlia,* Feb. 25, 1958, p. 3; Jan. 23, 1960, p. 3).*

Yet, without an improvement in material conditions and a reduced compulsion to steal, it seems unlikely that even the most elemental forms of self-service could be introduced. As the standard of living continues to improve, it is probable that much of the excessive zeal devoted to the

---

* Ideally, of course, there should be no such reluctance under a socialist system. When asked about reports that Soviet employees had refused to accept material responsibility, one Soviet department store executive responded by saying that no such situation could exist. Every Soviet trade employee was dedicated to the best service of the people and the employees would immediately see that brigade responsibility was the best system for all!

protection of state property will be unnecessary. This may permit the removal of some of the existing pressures, thereby allowing for more creativity and experimentation. This is a prerequisite for improved service and efficiency, especially in trade and distribution.

CONCLUSION

While the complexity of the problems created by the stewardship of public goods has diminished in recent years, there are still many impediments to efficiency. The controls of bureaucracy seem to hinder as much as they promote. It is in the use of material and psychological incentives, however, that the Russians appear to have made the most progress. The passage of time also brings with it a higher standard of living and therefore more flexibility in Soviet economic life. It will be interesting to see if service competition and improved efficiency develop as inventories begin to accumulate. Will it be necessary for manufacturers of consumers' goods to be more responsive to the requests of wholesalers who in turn are more concerned about pleasing retailers and consumers? Is it possible that better techniques of merchandising will become as important as more scientific marketing research?

While it seems likely that the problem of absentee ownership will remain a crucial one, delegated authority per se need not necessarily mean poor service or inefficiency. Despite the delegation of authority, service and efficiency in most of the chain stores of the West are still of a high quality. The issue, therefore, is whether or not service in the Soviet Union with such large-scale absentee ownership will be able to provide more adequately for its consumers, given the existing system of Soviet bureaucracy and incentives. Is it possible to strike a middle road between control and creativity? It will be interesting to see if this can be done without a radical change in goals.

[7] COSTS OF DISTRIBUTION

THUS FAR, little has been said about costs of distribution. Ordinarily, one would expect that before there can be any discussion about financial control, distribution expense should be analyzed. In the Soviet Union, however, it will be seen that the statistical definition of distribution costs is unique. Contrary to normal practice, it is difficult to discuss Soviet costs of distribution without having first explained the role and function of credit, markup, profit, and personnel in the Soviet system. Now that we have the necessary perspective, it is possible to evaluate the special significance of Soviet statistics for cost of distribution.

THE CHALLENGE OF SOVIET COSTS OF DISTRIBUTION

In the Soviet Union, the concept of cost of distribution has been surrounded with a certain mystique. The low level of Russian distribution costs is considered by Soviet economists as evidence of their superior marketing efficiency and another proof of the inherent advantage of a Socialist system.

> Costs of distribution in the Soviet Union are several times lower than they are under capitalism. . . . In capitalist countries, the overwhelming portion of labor expense in distribution is spent on merchandising the goods (*realizatsiia*), advertising, bookkeeping, etc. . . . Because of anarchy and competition, costs of distribution under capitalism frequently make up one half of the retail price (Birman, 1957, p. 220).

Retail costs of distribution in the Soviet Union in 1960 were officially reported to be 5.74 per cent of retail sales value. Total distribution costs of consumers' goods, which were said to be 7.53 per cent, were not much higher. (See Table 12.) In comparison, estimates of American costs of distribution usually run from 37–50 per cent of retail sales value. Thus, at first glance it does appear that the relative level of distribution costs in the United States is at least five times higher than it is in the Soviet Union.

Considering that Americans have traditionally felt their relative efficiency in the area of trade and distribution to be unchallenged, this reported low cost of Russian distribution activity should come as a surprise. To some extent the high American costs may be explained by the diverse forms of American ownership and the variation in domestic and international accounting procedures. Even if one makes allowance for this, however, there is still a significant difference between American and Russian distribution costs.

Equally unexpected, however, is the intensity with which the Russians berate themselves for not reducing costs of distribution below the present low levels. That there is considerable room for reducing costs of distribution in the Soviet Union is clear to anyone who has read self-criticism by Soviet officials or reports of foreign commentators. There seems to be universal agreement that distribution expense should be substantially lower. Every yearly plan and every discussion of marketing in the Soviet Union include ritualized calls for Soviet employees and managers to reduce distribution costs by means of increased productivity and by more efficient work. If Soviet costs of distribution (as we interpret the concept) are actually only 7 or 8 per cent of retail sales, such *outspoken* dissatisfaction with existing performance would seem out of place.

Confronted with such a paradox, the meaning of cost of distribution in the Soviet Union as represented by the official Soviet statistics must be examined carefully. It is necessary to determine accurately just what cost data cover in the Soviet Union and to adjust Soviet figures so a meaningful comparison can be made with the distribution cost information collected in the United States.

The first objective of this chapter, therefore, is to determine how the Russian concept of distribution cost at the manufacturing, wholesaling, and retailing stages compares with the corresponding concept in American data. It will be seen that while most major costs are properly accounted for, some correction is none the less necessary. Adjustment must be made for profit margins, sales taxes, wholesale costs, and *kolkhoz* (collective farm) market costs before a meaningful comparison can be made of total distribution markup in the Soviet Union and in the United States. Allowance for these items triples and quadruples the size of Russian distribution markup.

However, even though this allowance reduces the dif-

Table 12—Costs of Distribution in Soviet Trade,* Unadjusted (in Prices of Respective Year)

	1940	1950	1955	1956	1957	1958	1959	1960
Total (in million rubles)	1,909	3,286	4,089	4,246	4,693	4,949	5,308	5,807
Wholesaling	210	554	575	532	567	585	617	640
Retailing	1,250	2,098	2,646	2,827	3,158	3,357	3,643	4,023
Restaurants	449	633	868	886	967	1,007	1,048	1,144
As a per cent of sales volume of specific branch:								
Wholesaling	1.77	1.64	1.34	1.18	1.16	1.06	1.04	1.04
Retailing	8.21	6.78	6.06	5.88	5.71	5.59	5.68	5.74
Restaurants	19.63	13.35	14.76	14.67	15.33	15.65	16.27	16.29
As a per cent of retail sales (including restaurant sales):	10.90	9.21	8.26	7.84	7.61	7.44	7.52	7.53
Wholesaling	1.20	1.55	1.16	0.98	0.92	0.88	0.87	.83
Retailing	7.14	5.88	5.34	5.22	5.12	5.05	5.16	5.22
Restaurants	2.56	1.78	1.76	1.64	1.57	1.51	1.49	1.48
As a per cent of total costs of distribution:								
Wholesaling	11	17	14	12	12	12	11.5	11
Retailing	66	64	65	67	67	68	68.5	69
Restaurants	23	19	21	21	21	20	20	20
Total	100	100	100	100	100	100	100	100

SOURCE: TsSU 3, p. 760; TsSU 5, p. 709.

* Percentages are calculated from sales volume net of commission sales.

ference between Soviet and American distribution costs, there is still a significant gap. Further analysis suggests that some marketing operations in the United States are indeed significantly more costly than in the Soviet Union. Yet the lack of customer service and adequate marketing facilities in the Soviet Union would seem to be the major explanation for the Russian cost advantage. In a final attempt to assess the relative efficiency of the two systems, a comparison of retail sales per employee indicates that sales per Russian retail employee are at best only slightly higher, if not actually lower, than sales per American salesclerk.

A COMPARISON OF RUSSIAN
AND AMERICAN DISTRIBUTION MARKUP DATA

American Markup Data

While this chapter is primarily concerned with the meaningfulness of Soviet distribution costs, it is first necessary to point out certain limitations in the American cost data. There are no official government statistics of distribution markup in the United States. Furthermore, because of the variation in business ownership and accounting procedures, private estimates are usually subject to considerable variation. One of the most recent studies prepared by Harold Barger for the National Bureau of Economic Research indicates that the marketing markup in the United States is 37 per cent of the retail value, about 8 per cent of which is value added by wholesalers (Barger, 1955, p.

25). While this includes some transportation cost, Barger indicates that more complete coverage would raise distribution markup in the United States from the minimum of 37 per cent to something less than 50 per cent. The higher figure more nearly approximates an earlier estimate by Paul Stewart and J. Dewhurst published by the Twentieth Century Fund (Stewart and Dewhurst, 1939, p. 119). Despite the various shortcomings, it seems fair to say that the average marketing markup in the United States from the manufacturer to the retailer ranges between 37–50 per cent.

Russian Manufacturing and Wholesaling Costs of Distribution

Statistical information about official Russian cost of distribution figures is more readily available. Government sources provide data going back to the years before World War II. None the less, information regarding costs of distribution at the manufacturing and wholesaling levels in the Soviet Union is sketchy. Distribution costs incurred by the manufacturer of consumers' goods apparently are included in the statistics as a wholesaling expense. Consequently, there are no separate figures for distribution costs of manufacturers. An exception is the expenditure arising from the procurement of agricultural products and their initial processing, as well as the distribution cost of other manufacturers not producing finished consumers' goods. Exactly how much should be added to Russian figures in order to compensate for this omission by the Russians is unclear. One Russian writer intimates that such expenses total 5.3 billion rubles, but this figure certainly seems excessive

(Bakanov, 1959, p. 20; Gogol', 1960, p. 345). None the less, any comparison of American and Russian distribution costs in wholesaling will require the inclusion of some figure in addition to the normally stated wholesale fee of 600 million rubles. (See Table 16.)

The main components of Soviet wholesaling expense consists of wages of warehouse and distribution personnel and of expenses for storage and transportation. Since almost all Soviet manufactured items are sold FOB destination, transportation accounts for the largest proportion of distribution expense prior to the retail operation. From 56 to 65 per cent of total wholesale expenditures go for the movement of goods (Abaturov, 1956, pp. 42-43; Gogol', 1960, p. 350).*

Russian Retailing Costs of Distribution

Differences in the definition of costs make the comparison of distribution expense potentially more troublesome at the retail level. The meaningfulness of Soviet retail prices and costs has been the subject of much discussion both inside and outside the Soviet Union. While there are many aspects to the debate, we are concerned here only with those factors and practices that affect retail costs of distribution and the relation of distribution cost to total retail sales value.

Examination of the Russian categories of retail expense shown in Table 13 will lead to some question about Russian cost-setting practices. Because of arbitrary and sudden changes, it is necessary to ascertain whether or not all the

---

* This was also true before the transfer of wholesale organizations to the Ministry of Trade in 1953 (Gatovskii, 1955, p. 460).

major cost factors in distribution are accurately reflected in Russian calculations.

Rate-Making Practice. Upon close analysis of Soviet distribution costs, the reader is struck by certain large and sudden revisions of the distribution charges (Abaturov, 1956, pp. 61, 72, 142, 147; Gatovskii, 1955, pp. 35, 47, 244, 256; Gogol', 1958, pp. 156, 236-46). Undoubtedly many adjustments reflect the increased or decreased cost of

Table 13—Structure of Costs of Distribution in Retail Trade in the USSR (as a Percentage of Retail Sales Volume and as a Percentage of Total Distribution in Prices of the Given Year)

	1932		1937		1940		1950	
Total costs of distribution	11.31	100	9.40	100	8.21	100	6.78	100
Which consists of:								
Freight-auto, railroad, water	2.59	23	2.37	25	2.08	25	1.37	20
Salaries	3.53	31	2.60	28	2.51	31	2.42	36
Rent and maintenance of premises and equipment	0.92	8	0.88	9	0.78	10	0.77	12
Repairs	0.26	2	0.39	4	0.32	4	0.20	3
Finishing, packaging, reprocessing, storage, icing	0.21	2	0.18	2	0.17	2	0.16	2
Interest	0.33	3	0.30	3	0.20	2	0.59	9
Commodity wastage and spoilage	0.35	3	0.71	8	0.38	5	0.29	4
Net expense from packaging waste	0.23	2	0.36	4	0.18	2	0.10	1
Administrative expense of senior organizations	2.05	18	0.69	7	0.75	9	0.28	4
Other	0.84	8	0.92	10	0.84	10	0.60	9

SOURCE: TsSU 3, pp. 762–63; TsSU 5, p. 710.

performing certain services. None the less, while it may be expected that the cost of various services and materials will change periodically, the magnitude of some of the changes suggests that rates are often manipulated for noneconomic reasons. In fact, it has been admitted that the primary motive behind some of the changes has been simply to reduce costs of distribution in trade (Lisitsian, 1957, p. 38).

An example of one of the most extreme cases of rate manipulation is the lowering of electric rates on January 1, 1951, from 25 kopecks to only 6 kopecks per kilowatt hour. Over the years, this move reportedly reduced distribution costs by almost 100 million rubles (Abaturov, 1956,

1955		1956		1957		1958		1959		1960	
6.06	100	5.88	100	5.71	100	5.59	100	5.68	100	5.74	100
1.29	21	1.21	21	1.15	20	1.12	20	1.16	20	1.18	21
2.16	36	2.10	36	2.12	37	2.07	37	2.15	38	2.15	37
0.69	11	0.69	12	0.67	12	0.67	12	0.71	13	0.71	12
0.18	3	0.14	2	0.14	2	0.13	2	0.13	2	0.13	2
0.15	2	0.15	3	0.14	2	0.14	3	0.14	2	0.14	2
0.24	4	0.27	5	0.27	5	0.27	5	0.31	5	0.33	6
0.27	5	0.28	5	0.27	5	0.27	5	0.27	5	0.27	5
0.12	2	0.12	2	0.12	2	0.12	2	0.12	2	0.12	2
0.44	7	0.44	7	0.38	7	0.36	6	0.24	4	0.22	4
0.52	9	0.48	7	0.45	8	0.44	8	0.45	8	0.49	9

p. 73).* Considering the subsequent shortages of electric power, a rate reduction of this size was not economically justified. None the less, in terms of total costs of distribution the over-all effect of such manipulations seems minor. Consequently, no compensating adjustment in the data is necessary at this point.

THE MAKE-UP AND RELATIVE IMPORTANCE OF RETAIL DISTRIBUTION

Expenses

Surprisingly, the coverage of economic costs in retailing in the Soviet Union and the United States is very similar. Not only is there no need for undue concern about the arbitrary costing practices in the Soviet Union, but ideological factors do not seem to be important. While the practice is not the same in other sectors of the economy, it will be seen that the Russians do include rent, short-term interest, and advertising in their calculation of distribution cost.

The attempt to compare the structure of distribution costs in the United States and the USSR is again hampered by the lack of official data in the former. Furthermore, there is such a disparity in costs between stores of different size and purpose that whatever data are used usually repre-

---

* Since the state is the owner of the enterprise providing the distribution network with its services, the state can manipulate service and material charges within wide limits.

sent no more than one point on a possible range of costs. Bearing this in mind, the best studies of American costs for this purpose seem to be those published by the Harvard Business School under the direction of Malcolm P. McNair, H. Lawrence Isaacson, and Wilbur B. England (England, 1961; Isaacson, 1961). These surveys are compiled yearly for food chains and department and specialty stores. The relation of various major expenses to total cost in 1960 for these three major types of outlets is shown in Table 14.

While caution is necessary when making a comparison of relative distribution costs between the two countries, several noteworthy features emerge from Tables 13 and 14. First, as mentioned above, the Russians do include such doctrinally suspect items as rent, interest, and advertising. Surprisingly, relative property expenses are approximately equal in the two countries. Both figures include rent, amortization charges, insurance, appliance and fixture costs, and current repairs and upkeep. The large amount spent on maintenance and amortization seems to account for the major part of Soviet rent expense.

As for relative interest charges, the proportion of interest to total cost of distribution is also about equal in the two countries despite the fact that the Russians do not make any explicit charge for interest on fixed capital in the Soviet Union. Retail interest charges on short-term working capital amount to 6 per cent of total distribution costs in the Soviet Union. This seems to equal the combined long-term and short-term interest charges in the United States, which are imputed in Table 14. One explanation may be that a large portion of capital in American firms is contributed as equity capital and that inventory turnover in the United States is faster (Campbell, Sept., 1958, p.

Table 14—Relative Costs of Distribution for American Food Chains, Department and Specialty Stores in 1960 Compared with Relative Costs of Distribution for All Outlets at the Retail Level in the Soviet Union in 1960 (Figures in Per Cent of Total Distribution Cost, Profit Excluded)

| | AMERICAN | | | SOVIET |
	Food Chains	Department Stores	Specialty Stores	Retail Trade
Payroll	49 ab	51 ab	48 ab	37
Transportation	6 a	4 a	4 a	21
Real estate and equipment	20 a	12	13	14
Advertising	11	8	8	0.4
Interest	2	6 c	5 c	6
Services purchased	—	4 a	3 a	—
Supplies	5 a	6	6 a	—
Other	7	9	13	22
Total	100	100	100	100

SOURCE: American data: England, 1961, pp. 8, 29; Isaacson, 1961, pp. 13, 28, 111, 154.
    Soviet data: TsSU 5, p. 710; TsSU 6, p. 122.
    a. Since the Harvard Business School studies do not list transportation as a separate category, it is necessary to make adustments in the American data if the material is to be comparable with the Soviet information. This can be done by referring to the classification called "Expenses by Functional Divisions" (England, 1961, p. 29) and "Expense Center Trends" (Isaacson, 1961, pp. 13, 111, 154). For department stores, approximately 60 per cent of transportation expense is otherwise classified as Services Purchased, and the remainder as Payroll. The same type of readjustment is necessary in the food chain breakdown and for specialty stores.
    b. Includes payroll taxes.
    c. Interest is partly imputed.

549). The inventory build-up that has taken place in recent years also explains the increase in interest expense in 1960. This increase was also a reflection of the added expenses connected with installment credit, which was inaugurated in 1959.

Of a different magnitude is the relative expense for advertising in the Soviet Union. Since advertising costs arise as a result of human action and not from the economic nature of things, as is the case with property and capital expense, we should expect that advertising costs would be a smaller fraction of total costs in the Soviet Union. None the less, the very existence of an expense category for advertising in the Soviet Union requires a second look.

Until now, the Russians have released no advertising statistics except for the years 1952 and 1955 (TsSU 6, pp. 122-23; Bakanov, 1959, p. 37). Consequently, a comparison of American and Russian advertising costs has been very difficult. However, Soviet authorities have supplemented these data with other information. In 1959, T. S. Stepaniants, the director of Torgreklama, the adver-

Table 15—Retail Advertising Expense in the Soviet Union for Selected Years *

Year (1)	Ruble Expenditure (millions) (2)	As a Percentage of Retail Sales (3)
1940	2.17	0.03
1951	2.79	0.02
1952	3.25	0.02
1953	3.9	0.02
1954	—	—
1955	—	0.02
1956	—	0.02
1959	14.2	—

SOURCE: Report of American Marketing Delegation to the Soviet Union, 1960, p. 40. This information with the above blanks was shown to the writer by A. Fefilov, the Director of the Plekhanov Institute. The reader should compare this information with that published in TsSU 6, pp. 122—23. This shows that retail advertising expense in 1955 amounted to 7 million rubles, of which 4.5 were for the Ministry of Trade outlets only. Added to the 7-million figure was a 0.5-million ruble expenditure by restaurants.

* The data apparently refer only to the activities of the Ministry of Trade and exclude the advertising expense of restaurants, consumer cooperatives, and other retail operations.

tising agency of the RSFSR, told this writer that he estimated total advertising expenditures in his republic to be
about 25 million rubles. This may be an overstatement. In
1960, this author was shown the data in Table 15. This
table indicates advertising expenses in the Soviet Union
for certain selected years in ruble terms and/or as a percentage of total retail sales. There is some uncertainty,
however, about how the data in Table 15 are related to the
previously published information about advertising costs.
It appears that Table 15 covers only the sales activities of
the Ministry of Trade, which is only 50 per cent of total
retail sales. Excluded, therefore, are the advertising costs
of restaurants, cooperative stores, company stores (the
ORS), and the Ministries of Health and Communication,
which operate the drugstores and newspaper stands.* If
this assumption is correct, it is likely that until 1956 relative advertising expense approximated 0.33 per cent of
total distribution cost, or 0.02 per cent of retail sales volume. Of course this is much lower than the advertising
expenses of either American food chain stores or department stores, which was, respectively, 11 per cent and 8 per
cent of total retail costs.

Because of the ambiguity of the Russian data, no un-
qualified statement seems possible, but there does seem to
be an indication that relative advertising costs in 1959

---

* The ruble data in column 2 of Table 15 is consistent with the
percentage data in column 3 only if the "retail sales" covered in column
3 consist of 50 per cent of total retail sales, exclusive of restaurant
activity. This happens to be the approximate share of the sales of
stores under the Ministry of Trade to total retail sales (TsSU 6, p. 36).
Only in this way do the data shown the author seem related to the
published data. Thus, the 1959 estimate given the author by Stepaniants
could be a correct figure of combined costs.

increased. If it is true that the 14.2 million rubles spent for advertising applied only to 50 per cent of the sales volume of Russian state stores, exclusive of restaurant sales, then it appears that relative advertising costs have increased to 0.04 per cent of retail sales volume. Although this is still insignificant in comparison with American advertising costs, a trend in the direction of increased advertising expense seems to support some conclusions to be presented in Chapter 8.

One other important difference in the structure of relative costs should be noted. Despite the fact that the largest share of transportation expense is borne by Soviet manufacturers and wholesalers who ship their goods FOB destination, transportation costs of Soviet retailers account for approximately 20 per cent of retail costs; it is even higher for cooperative stores in rural areas. In the United States where goods are also shipped FOB destination, a comparable figure for food chains and department stores is, at most, 6 per cent.

While relative transportation charges are high, relative wage payments are low. In the United States, labor costs amount to almost 50 per cent of operating costs, while in the Soviet Union wages and salaries constitute no more than 40 per cent. Unless retail transportation cost in the Soviet Union consists primarily of wages, the resulting implication is that labor is much less important in the socialist marketing system of the Soviet Union than it is in the United States.

Thus far, despite differences in relative importance and the omission of long-term interest charges in the USSR, the accounting coverage for various distribution expenses in the Soviet Union and the United States appears to be very similar. Although it seems fair to say that procedures for the determination of retail cost may be quite arbitrary in the Soviet Union, there do not appear to be major defects in the cost categories officially presented by the Russians. It is true, of course, that the relative size of certain accounting costs in the United States and the Soviet Union is not the same and that marketing in the Soviet Union is less a matter of advertising and personal service than it is in the United States. Furthermore, there are still adjustments to be made in the next section. None the less, there is no major reason that the differing accounting procedures should adversely affect the comparisons between the two countries.

Marketing Markup as a Percentage of Sales Volume

Having investigated the significance of the various cost components in the Soviet Union and their relation to American counterparts, we are now ready to compare marketing markups as a percentage of sales in each country. The revised estimate of marketing markup in the Soviet Union is shown in Table 16. The average adjusted markup is increased to approximately 20–30 per cent of retail price as compared with the officially published figure of 7–8 per cent. It can be seen that even though the American distribution markup remains larger than the Soviet figure, the difference is more like two to one rather than the five-to-one, or higher, ratios often claimed by those in the Soviet Union.

Having spelled out the conclusions of the analysis, it is now necessary to explain how the results in Table 16

Table 16—Derivation of Adjusted Markup/Sales Ratio for Soviet Wholesale and Retail Trade in 1960 (in Billion Rubles)

Column 1		Column 2	
Retail Sales Volume (adjusted)		Distribution Markup (adjusted)	
ITEM	RUBLES	ITEM	RUBLES
Adjusted retail sales	67.8	**Retail**	
Adjusted restaurant sales	6.9	Retail store markup	5.3
		Restaurant markup	1.2
Total retail and restaurant sales	74.7	Total retail and restaurant markup	6.5
Less turnover tax adjusted at rate of 40 per cent	29.9	**Wholesale**	
		Wholesale cost of distribution	0.6
		Profit of wholesalers	0.2
Total retail and restaurant sales net of turnover tax	44.8	Cost of procurement and other distribution activities in the Soviet Union	1.0 — 5.3
Plus collective farm market sales	3.6		
Total adjusted sales figure	48.4	Profit of procurement and other distribution activities in the Soviet Union	0.4
		Total wholesale markup	2.2 — 6.5
		Collective Farm Markets	0.4 — 1.0
		Total markup	9.1 — 14

$\dfrac{\text{Column 2}}{\text{Column 1}}$ equals a wholesale-retail distribution markup of almost 20–30 per cent.

were derived. First, it must be noted that Table 16 is presented in terms of the markup/sales ratio, not just as a ratio of cost of distribution/sales. Most of the American-Russian comparisons that have been published by the Russians in the past have not been consistent about this. Invariably the Russians will select a cost of distribution figure from Table 12 for their part of the comparison and then proceed to contrast it with the American figure of 37–50 per cent, which represents *total markup*—that is, cost of distribution *plus* profit. This obviously places American figures at a considerable disadvantage. Consequently, a more consistent comparison is called for to include retail and wholesale profit margins and eliminate the impact of the extremely large Soviet sales tax. To do this, two basic adjustments in the Russian data are necessary. The first, as carried out in column 1 of Table 16, is to derive a sales volume figure to which may be applied the ruble value of the distribution markup. This involves the adjustment of official sales volume to make it suitable for use with the available markup data. From this figure it is then necessary to subtract the turnover tax, which otherwise inflates the volume of retail sales. With a workable sales volume estimate, it is then possible to make the second basic adjustment. This consists of determining a factory-to-consumer markup figure as shown in column 2 of Table 16. This task here will be to consider additional wholesaling costs, as well as the operating cost, of the collective farm markets.

If the observer attempts to analyze distribution costs net of profit as the Russians do, he may suffer from a variety of misconceptions. If only cost of distribution is considered (profit margin is ignored), it will appear that the ratio of

Table 17—Markup (Cost of Distribution Plus Profit) for Retail Trade Enterprises of the Union Republic Trade Ministries, ORS, Supply Bases (Prodsnab) and Consumer Cooperatives (Unadjusted) (in Prices of Corresponding Year)

YEAR	Retail Trade			Restaurants		
	MARKUP	COST OF DISTRIBUTION	PROFIT	MARKUP	COST OF DISTRIBUTION	PROFIT
			Billion Rubles			
1940	1.375	1.050	0.325	0.495	0.378	0.117
1950	2.228	1.763	0.465	0.659	0.607	0.052
1951	2.374	1.832	0.542	0.731	0.641	0.090
1952	2.528	1.919	0.609	0.796	0.673	0.123
1953	2.974	2.181	0.793	0.871	0.724	0.147
1954	3.444	2.443	1.001	0.968	0.823	0.145
1955	3.476	2.365	1.111	1.002	0.838	0.164
1956	3.796	2.519	1.277	1.004	0.850	0.154
1957	4.343	2.891	1.452	1.086	0.948	0.138
1958	4.662	3.089	1.573	1.122	0.987	0.135
1959	4.916	3.337	1.579	1.134	1.021	0.113
1960	5.258	3.695	1.563	1.219	1.121	0.098
			Percentage of Retail Sales			
1940	10.70	8.17	2.53	23.02	17.92	5.10
1950	8.16	6.46	1.70	14.56	13.41	1.15
1951	8.37	6.46	1.91	15.30	13.41	1.89
1952	8.59	6.52	2.07	15.67	13.25	2.42
1953	8.81	6.46	2.35	15.76	13.10	2.66
1954	8.81	6.25	2.56	16.74	14.22	2.52
1955	8.43	5.74	2.69	17.65	14.78	2.87
1956	8.35	5.54	2.81	17.27	14.63	2.64
1957	8.13	5.41	2.72	17.51	15.29	2.22
1958	8.01	5.31	2.70	17.78	15.64	2.14
1959	7.93	5.38	2.55	17.97	16.18	1.79
1960	7.76	5.45	2.31	17.74	16.31	1.43

SOURCE: TsSU 5, p. 712.

distribution cost to total retail sales in the Soviet Union has fallen almost constantly from 1940 to 1958. (See Table 17.) Further analysis reveals, however, that the fall in cost of distribution has frequently been offset by an increase in the profit rate of the retailer. Such conditions prevailed from 1950 to 1956. The net effect was that total marketing markup during that period almost always increased and, until 1957, did not fully reflect the lower costs of distribution.

If an international comparison of distribution expenses is to be made, profit margins in both countries must be included in the analysis. What profit margin information the Russians have made available is shown in Table 17. Unfortunately, if these data are to be used, several preliminary adjustments must be made. This is necessary in order to obtain an estimate of Russian retail sales volume that will be consistent with the markup data made available by Russian statisticians.

As often happens with Soviet statistics, the distribution costs of the outlets listed in the caption of Table 17—that is, those of the Republic Ministries of Trade, company stores (ORS), supply bases (Prodsnab), and consumer cooperatives—do not encompass all the retail costs of distribution normally included in total retail trade. Consequently, there are major differences between the costs of distribution shown in Table 12 (which covers all distribution outlets) and those in Table 17 (which covers the most important, but selected, outlets mentioned above). For example, in 1940 the cost of distribution of all retail stores (exclusive of restaurants) as reported in Table 12 was 1.25 billion rubles, but the cost of distribution of the outlets of all the Republic Trade Ministries, the company

stores, supply bases, and consumer cooperatives cited in
Table 17 was only 1.05 billion rubles. Such differences
have persisted. In 1960, the cost of distribution of all stores
equaled 4.02 billion rubles, while for the most select group
in Table 17, it was only 3.70 billion.

To some extent, these differences may be due to the
omission of various administrative expenses. Whatever the
reason, this unexplained disparity in the data makes it
necessary to construct a new set of retail sales figures if
the markup data (which are only available in the form
presented in Table 17) are to be of use. Only by recon-
structing and adjusting the magnitude of total retail sales
is it possible to establish a valid relationship between total
sales and the total markup figures. This adjustment can be
made by relating the more select cost of distribution figure,
expressed in rubles, to the appropriate cost of distribution
figure expressed as a percentage of retail sales:

$$\frac{3.7 \text{ billion rubles}}{x} = \frac{5.45\%}{100\%}$$

Both of these figures are given in Table 17. With this information we can derive a retail volume of 67.8 billion
rubles. The comparable sales volume for restaurants after
adjustment is 6.9 billion rubles. As shown in column 1 of
Table 16, this results in a total retail and restaurant sales
volume of 74.7 billion rubles.

In comparing Soviet and American distribution costs,
it is equally important that adjustments be made for the
unusually large sales tax levied in the Soviet Union. This
charge, the turnover tax, is applied at the wholesale level

to the factory price and is regarded as part of the total wholesale cost by the retailer. Information about specific sales or turnover tax rates in the Soviet Union is largely unobtainable. However, the average rate of all turnover tax collections to retail and restaurant sales volume was approximately 40 per cent in 1960; in earlier years it has been as high as 65 per cent (TsSU 5, pp. 681, 843).* While there are sales and excise taxes in the United States, the rate is usually no more than 3 per cent.

This difference in the size of sales taxes has an important effect on the analysis of relative distribution costs. It means that the sales volume against which the Russian cost of distribution is measured is much higher than it would be in the absence of such a tax. Consequently, the resulting cost of distribution as a percentage of retail sales will appear to be considerably lower than it is where the tax is smaller. For example, if cost of distribution amounts to 5 rubles, and retail sales including turnover tax are 100, then the cost of distribution is only 5 per cent of retail sales; but if retail sales volume net of taxes actually equalled 50 rubles, the 5 rubles expended as a cost of distribution would be 10 per cent of retail sales.

Furthermore, because the turnover tax is applied to the post-tax price, not the pretax price as in the United States, the effect of a 40 per cent turnover tax is much greater than it first appears. A 40 per cent turnover tax on the final sales (or post-tax) price means a larger absolute amount of tax per item than if taxes were 40 per cent of the pretax price. To illustrate, assume a product nor-

---

* To some extent the turnover tax may be a disguised factor cost. A small portion of the turnover tax is also levied on nonconsumers' goods, primarily petroleum products.

mally sells for 100 rubles with no sales tax. In the United States, a 40 per cent sales tax would be imposed on the pretax price of 100 rubles. This results in a tax of 40 rubles, so that the item would ultimately sell for 140 rubles. In the Soviet Union, however, a 40 per cent tax means that the 40 per cent figure is applied to the *final* sales (post-tax) price. Thus, a 40 per cent sales tax in the Soviet Union really means that the original 100-ruble good would sell for 166 rubles 67 kopecks. In the Soviet Union the 40 per cent tax is applied to the 166-ruble 67-kopeck price, not the 100-ruble price. The consequence is a tax of 66 rubles and 67 kopecks (instead of the usual 40 rubles), which is 40 per cent of the final sales or post-tax price. The application of the turnover tax to the post-tax figure in this way by the Russians increases the markup over cost considerably more than a similar Western tax.

Clearly the Russian turnover tax tends to exaggerate the sales volume of the goods actually sold. This, in turn, leads to an understatement of costs of distribution as a percentage of sales volume. If distribution markup figures in the Soviet Union are to be compared with the United States, where the sales tax is considerably less and applied differently, sales volume figures in the Soviet Union must be taken net of sales taxes. Thus, we make another adjustment in our comparison of Russian and American distribution costs. Applying the average turnover tax rate of 40 per cent to the adjusted retail and restaurant sales figure of 74.7 billion rubles in Table 16, we obtain an adjusted retail and restaurant sales figure of 44.8 billion rubles net of taxes. If to this is added the sum of untaxed sales on the collective farm markets, we derive an over-all sales volume of 48.4 billion rubles.

Having obtained a workable sales volume figure and having deducted from it the turnover tax, the first phase of the calculation is completed; now there is a base for comparison. The next task is to obtain a figure for total distribution markup. The statistical shortcomings in the Soviet data were presented earlier. While there is room for improvement, there is no cause to reject the general validity of the official markup statistics reproduced in Table 17. The figures of 5.3 billion rubles for stores and 1.2 billion rubles for restaurants as shown in Table 16 seem to be fair representations of the markup in government and cooperative retail stores and restaurants.

Having selected a figure for retail markup, we can now proceed to derive one for wholesale markup. In the Soviet statistical handbook for 1960, costs of distribution of wholesale trade organizations are listed as 640 million rubles and their profit is given as 240 million rubles (TsSU 5, pp. 709, 713). In addition, there are other organizations that perform wholesale activities in the Soviet Union. These include agricultural procurement agencies and some industrial marketing organizations. The Soviet economist, M. I. Bakanov, says that the total sum of such operations amounts to as much as 5.3 billion rubles a year (Bakanov, 1959, p. 21). Some of what he classifies as wholesaling, however, would be considered manufacturing expense in the United States. Consequently, to remind the reader of the statistical pitfalls involved in an analysis of this nature, a more cautious estimate is also presented in Table 16. For the more conservative end of the cost range, a figure of 1 billion rubles is used. This was derived by first calculating the approximate ratio of profit margin to cost of distribution for other trade organizations. Then this ratio was applied to the profit margin of these special wholesale organizations, which the yearly statistical handbook says is 400 million rubles (TsSU 5, p. 713).

One last and even more speculative adjustment is required. In the Soviet Union, the *kolkhoz* (collective farm) market is one of the main sources of fresh food. Resembling our farmers' markets, the collective farm markets, it will be remembered, sell as much as 14 per cent of certain foods, and a few years ago they sold over 20 per cent of these items. Estimates of the exact cost of collective farm market operation vary, but some Russian economists have suggested that total retail costs of distribution are raised by another 1–1.5 percent; that is, costs are increased from 5.74 to about 6.7–7.2 per cent of retail sales volume. This would mean costs of distribution in Table 16 would be adjusted upward by at least 10 per cent, or 400 million rubles (Bakanov, April, 1957, p. 16). Elsewhere the same economist has estimated that the cost of operating the collective farm markets is even higher and amounts to 1 billion rubles a year (Bakanov, 1959, p. 20). In our adjustment, we will assume that the marketing costs incurred by the collective farm markets run between 400 million and 1 billion rubles. If there was some means of estimating the indirect costs that arise when each day 700,000 peasants leave the land and become salesclerks, the upward revision would be much higher (*Sovetskaia Torgovlia,* Dec. 2, 1961, p. 1).

The result of all these adjustments, as shown in Table 16, is an estimate of the wholesale-retail markup that ranges from 9 to 14 billion rubles. When applied to a retail sales base of approximately 48 billion rubles, Table 16 shows that the Soviet markup (before taxes) from the wholesale level to the sales point is increased from the officially cited figure of 7.53 per cent to almost 20–30 per cent. This compares to 37–50 per cent for the United States. While other corrections undoubtedly could be made, the adjusted figures appear to represent a much more accurate picture of actual costs than the officially cited data.

SIGNIFICANCE OF LOWER COSTS
OF DISTRIBUTION IN THE SOVIET UNION
AS A MEASURE OF PRODUCTIVITY

While there is some satisfaction in showing that Russian costs are not that much lower after all, it is clear that there is still a significant difference between Russian and American costs of distribution. Two questions therefore arise: what is the explanation for this gap, and do the lower Russian costs indicate that the Russian distribution system is more efficient?

In answer to the first question, one must say that American costs of distribution are high. Moreover, there is undoubtedly considerable waste in the American marketing system. Certainly an annual advertising expenditure of $11–12 billion is hard to justify in its entirety. Moreover, in the United States there is duplication in both goods and outlets.

Yet the gap in Soviet and American costs of distribution is not explained solely by waste in American marketing practices. On the one hand, the Russians have also been unable to eliminate waste and redudancy in their distribution process (Vasilenko and Sushko, June, 1959, p. 40; M. Bespalov, Mar., 1960, p. 22), and on the other, they appear to be far behind the United States in introducing improved marketing methods. The explanation, if there is one, may be more easily perceived if the availability of facilities and services in the Soviet Union is considered.

Candid Soviet marketing officials have recognized that one of the best explanations for the disparity in Russian and American distribution costs is not so much the duplication of services in the United States, but the absence of many services in the Soviet Union. As a Leningrad trade official explained to me, "Our service is inferior to yours. We have fewer stores, fewer clerks, and, as a result, lower costs of distribution!"

If, because of the absence of alternatives, the consumer can be compelled to stand in line, then it is clear that low costs of distribution are possible. Instead of a large number of elaborately designed stores and a staff of salesclerks, one clerk behind a dimly lit counter or stall will be sufficient to transfer the necessary merchandise to the long-suffering customer. The endless queues found everywhere in the Soviet Union are an indication that poor service may indeed be one explanation of the lower Russian cost of distribution.*

The reduction of distribution costs relative to retail sales after 1954 is to some extent a reflection of this re-

---

* Similarly, the marketing margin in India is reported to be 15 per cent of retail price. Yet few would insist that this indicates that the Indians have an efficient marketing system (Ralph Westfall and Harper W. Boyd, Jr., "Marketing in India," *Journal of Marketing*, Oct., 1960, p. 11).

duced service. Although retail sales from 1952 to 1960 have grown by more than 200 per cent, the number of retail outlets has increased by only 30 per cent *(Bakinskii Rabochii,* June 11, 1960, p. 2). The effect of this, naturally, has been that costs of distribution in relation to sales have fallen. Consequently, lower costs of distribution per se are not necessarily a good thing. There must be some assurance that service is not neglected in the process. Unfortunately, it is difficult to devise statistical measures for judging the quality of service. Thus, when we make comparisons between costs of distribution, it is all but impossible to determine whether or not the consumer is obtaining the same product (the goods plus service) for his money.

For a variety of reasons, therefore, it may be that cost of distribution and markup are not always the best criteria for judging efficiency in distribution. Not only are the costs often arbitrarily determined, but intangible factors are sometimes ignored. Consequently, it might be worth while to consider another measure of distribution efficiency.

While some of the above objections may remain as to its meaningfulness, a comparison of sales per employee in the respective countries may provide further information about the relative productivity and efficiency of the distribution systems in the United States and the Soviet Union.* Although there are many statistical and contextual shortcomings (the incomparability of American and Russian employment and sales data, the questionability of using a dollar/ruble ratio for this purpose, the inability of Russian salesclerks to obtain the proper delivery from suppliers, and the variability of the service offered in the respective

---

* This approach was suggested by Abram Bergson.

countries), the results are surprising. Considering the lack of service in the Soviet Union and the consequent customer turnover that should therefore be possible, it is logical to expect that productivity per employee in the Soviet Union would be higher than it is in the United States. It turns out that the contrary is often true.

To link American dollar retail sales and Russian ruble sales, we can use the dollar/ruble ratios compiled for the RAND Corporation by Norman Kaplan and Eleanor Wainstein (Kaplan and Wainstein, 1956, 1957). They concluded that the 1954 dollar/ruble ratio in 1950 American weights is 1.43 rubles to the dollar. With this ratio, one discovers in Table 18 that sales per employee in stores and restaurants combined was 80 per cent of that in the United States. Although the difference is not so striking, the more meaningful comparison of sales per employee in stores only also indicates greater efficiency in the United States. Including wholesale employees in such a comparison leads to the same result.

If, however, one of Kaplan's and Wainstein's alternative ratios is used, the results are somewhat more ambiguous. In this instance, by using 1954 Soviet weights, instead of 1950 American weights, a lower 1954 dollar/ruble ratio of 1.01 indicates that sales per employee in the Soviet Union are higher in one or two instances than in the United States. This prevents the formulation of any unreserved assertions. None the less, sales per employee often appear higher in American marketing than in the Soviet Union. Even where higher sales per employee are found in the Soviet Union, they are much less than one would expect from Russian statements about the differences in American and Russian distribution costs.

Table 18—Comparison of Sales per Worker in Russian and American Distribution Outlets

YEAR	STAGE OF DISTRIBUTION	Sales per Worker in the United States SALES VOLUME (in Millions of Dollars)	EMPLOYEES AND EMPLOYERS (thousands)	SALES PER PERSON (in Dollars)	Sales per Person IN RUBLES CONVERTED AT 1.01 Rubles to the Dollar	1.43
1954	Total retail sales	169,968	8,908	19,080	19,270	27,280
1958		199,646	9,730	20,519	20,720	29,340
1954	Including restaurant	13,101	1,720	7,618	7,690	10,890
1958		15,201	1,959	7,762	7,840	11,100
1954	Retail only	156,867	7,188	21,822	22,040	31,210
1958		184,445	7,771	23,734	23,970	33,940
1958	Total retail sales with wholesale employees added	199,646	12,688	15,700	15,860	22,450

SOURCE: U.S. Bureau of the Census, Statistical Abstract of the United States: 1960 (eighty-first edition), Washington, 1960, pp. 838–39, 847; TsSU 5, pp. 681, 708. Gogol', 1959, p. 311; TsSU 6, p. 113. The exchange rate of 1.01 is in Soviet weights and in terms of 1954 prices (An Addendum, p. 3). The 1.43 ratio is in 1950 American weights and in terms of 1954 prices (A Comparison, p. 28).

Sales per Worker in the Soviet Union			Sales of a Russian Worker Relative to an American Worker			
			AT EXCHANGE RATE OF 1.01	USSR ⎯⎯ US	AT EXCHANGE RATE OF 1.43	USSR ⎯⎯ US
SALES VOLUME (in Millions of Rubles)	EMPLOYEES (Thousands)	SALES PER PERSON (in Rubles)	(per cent)		(per cent)	
48.19	2,339	20,600	20,600 / 19,270	107	21,570 / 27,280	79
67.72	2,847	23,790	23,790 / 20,720	115	23,790 / 29,340	81
6.00	820	7,320	7,320 / 7,690	95	7,320 / 10,890	67
6.43	959	6,700	6,700 / 7,840	85	6,750 / 10,310	65
42.19	1,519	27,770	27,700 / 22,040	126	27,770 / 31,210	89
61.29	1,888	32,460	32,460 / 23,970	135	32,460 / 33,940	96
67.7	4,234	15,990	15,990 / 15,860	101	15,990 / 22,450	71

CONCLUSION

What is the conclusion to be drawn from the above analysis? After such contradictory results, if nothing else the assertion seems warranted that comparative measures of efficiency or productivity in distribution are not always consistent. Whether cost of distribution or sales per employee is the more appropriate index is all but impossible to determine.

While there is reason to believe that costs of distribution in the United States are higher than in the Soviet Union, the difference is more in the range of two to one rather than five to one as the Russians generally assert. However, the significance of even this adjusted figure is hard to judge. One reason for low costs of distribution in the Soviet Union is that service and convenience have been sacrificed. In spite of this, sales per employee in the Soviet Union appear to be unduly low.

Still unanswered is how the low sales per Russian employee can be reconciled with the low cost of distribution in the Soviet Union. Two possibilities suggest themselves: the first is that the ratio of wages to retail prices is much higher in the United States, and the second is that marketing in the United States uses relatively more capital, while marketing in the Soviet Union uses relatively more labor. The first condition indicates why costs in the Soviet Union are lower, and the second helps to explain the lower sales per Soviet clerk.

The Russians have recently become increasingly cognizant of the fact that service in Russian stores is inadequate and that their marketing efficiency is not as high as is usually implied by looking only at their official cost-of-distribution figures. There is a new awareness that satisfactory distribution demands not only the provision of goods but also service and efficiency. Toward this end, in 1959 and 1960, a significant increase in attention and capital was directed to the marketing sector. This has resulted in the first increase in the ratio of Soviet costs of distribution to retail sales since 1951.

As production of consumers' goods has increased, the Russians have discovered that it becomes more difficult to satisfy consumers' demands. In turn this has brought about a rise in costs related to merchandising and to promoting the sale of goods. The increased bookkeeping expenses required by the issuance of instalment credit, the expenses of advertising, and the larger working capital costs of carrying larger inventory stocks are typical. If in addition, service is improved and the number of outlets increased, costs will rise even higher in the future. Therefore, as more attention is devoted to merchandising, service, and efficiency, the Russians may find that customer satisfaction and sales per employee will increase but so will costs of distribution.

[8] *MARX, THE U.S.S.R., AND THE FUNCTIONS OF MARKETING*

TWO TASKS remain to be performed. The easiest and briefest will be a review of the highlights noted in the preceding chapters. The most complex and provocative will be an attempt to synthesize Marxist theory with what has been learned about trade and distribution in the Soviet Union. It is hoped that such an analysis will uncover some trends that will not only add to our knowledge about the past development of marketing in the Soviet Union but will suggest something about the future. Finally, it is also possible that from this will evolve a better appreciation of the over-all economic contribution of the marketing process.

RECAPITULATION

In each of the earlier chapters of this book, certain broad features were highlighted for the reader. It was first necessary to describe the organization of the marketing system and the chain of command from the urban and rural stores to the Ministry of Trade and Gosplan. The division of functions into retailing, wholesaling, and manufacturing was found to be similar to that of the West, although greater centralization and administrative control was found to exist in the Soviet Union.

In Chapter 3, the methods used to plan the distribution of consumers' goods was explained. It was shown that some of the more theoretical procedures have become inadequate. Increased reliance on decentralized decision-making and less interference by Moscow in ascertaining local demand conditions was noted.

The complicated interrelationships that must be confronted by price-makers in a centralized state society were analyzed in Chapter 4. With conditions subject to eternal change, unanticipated side effects appear to be inevitable, especially when all major decisions are made at the center. The turnover tax was found to be a convenient tool for coping with many of the problems that arise, particularly when demand conditions change. None the less, the use of differential turnover and profit tax rates was found to be inconsistent with the Marxist theory of value.

With some knowledge of the pricing procedure, it was possible to discuss the use of financial controls in Chapter 5. It was suggested that financial controls were essential in any society that produced in anticipation of consumption. With control by the state, it might be expected that financial planning and control in the Soviet Union would be particularly effective. However, deficiencies and lack of coordination were noted.

Some of the effects of poor coordination in planning were seen in Chapter 6. Entrusting private individuals with public goods resulted in the formation of bureaucratic institutions, which makes coordination even more difficult. Special control measures were often introduced that adversely affected standards of customer service.

In Chapter 7, a comparison of Russian and American costs of distribution was presented. Some adjustment of Soviet data was required before any meaningful comparison could be made. While American costs of distribution were found to be double those in the Soviet Union, analysis of customer service and sales per employee in the two countries suggested that the relative level of distribution costs was not the only important variable. Moreover, a trend toward new and possibly higher distribution expenses in the Soviet Union was also indicated.

AN ANALYSIS

Essentially, the above paragraphs have summarized the main features of marketing in the Soviet Union. By projecting this material against the Marxist attitude toward marketing, some interesting insights are obtained.

In the first chapter of this book, Karl Marx was shown to reflect the social critic's historic contempt for profit-making by nonproductive agencies. Accordingly, he felt that the possibility of social waste arose whenever anyone other than the manufacturer or the direct producer handled the goods and profited thereby. While the phenomena of advertising, product differentiation, and installment credit were as yet unimportant in Marx's mid-nineteenth century, such practices would be classed by him along with the parasitic functions of speculation and money-lending that he knew well.

It should therefore be expected that in the Soviet Union, where Marx's ideas are held in such high esteem, the intermediary's role would be held to a minimum. Since the state controls and operates all channels of distribution, it would be expected that the excesses and intermediary activities so strongly criticized by Marx would have been deemphasized, if not eliminated. From the preceding chapters, however, it has been shown that the links between the producer and consumer have become increasingly more indirect in the Soviet Union and that many of the more wasteful forms of marketing, such as advertising, trade fairs, and commission trade, are being used. Therefore, the fact that marketing activities in the Soviet Union are more important than ever and that other controversial marketing methods—such as installment credit and product differentiation—have been reintroduced must be explained. One method of doing this is to use a stage-of-growth framework.

Stages of Growth

In examining the evolution of marketing, it seems possible to postulate two developmental stages for most societies. Distribution at the primary stage involves the very basic functions of retailing and wholesaling, which seem to be indispensable in any but the most primitive societies.

In the primary stage, the population is largely agricultural and the standard of living is low. As the standard of living gradually improves, the wholesaling tasks of collection and redistribution and the retailing activity of direct selling are further supplemented by more sophisticated and specialized operations. In the secondary stage, there is a rapid increase in the importance and number of middlemen. Soon there is the problem of calculating and meeting the demand of consumers who suddenly have a chance to exercise their choice among several varieties of a given product and competing types of goods. The characteristics of these two stages and how they relate to Marxism and marketing in the Soviet Union will now be discussed in more detail.

Primary Stage. The distribution activities necessary in the primary stage are the ones that Marx would have found the least objectionable. While Marx felt that some aspects of the wholesaling function could be wasteful, he considered retailing to be a necessary concomitant of the division of labor in an industrialized society.

Retailing as it existed prior to Stalin's death was quite devoid of frills. Initially, the cooperative retail trade network was regarded as the highest form of socialist organization and therefore was stressed. By 1931, however, the Soviet state had completely nationalized all retailing and wholesaling activities and by the mid-1930's the retailing structure had settled into its present mold. The state store network was given a virtual monopoly of sales in urban areas, and the so-called cooperative store network was given monopoly powers in rural regions.

The wholesaling network in the Soviet Union has been a part of the administrative and operational superstructure of the government store and cooperative network. While there have been innumerable reorganizations of wholesale and administrative units, these changes have always conformed to a basic pattern in which control is exercised both vertically and horizontally. While periodically the degree of power exercised by the Ministry of Trade or Gosplan may be increased at the expense of the horizontal power of the regional and republic authorities, there has been no demise of the wholesaling function.

Having briefly recalled the organizational framework of what is here called the primary stage, it is now possible to discuss the reasons for asserting that the functions of retailing and wholesaling are essential. Despite innumerable reorganizations, the basic functions of direct sales, storage, and assembly have had to be undertaken. No matter what organizations were abolished, the functions of retailing and wholesaling could not be eliminated. While it is true that in some cases the work could be consolidated, it was often found that it was even impossible to do this. If elimination or consolidation of certain chores was attempted, it was sometimes discovered, as in the attempted elimination of some wholesale depots in the 1930's (see Appendix), that the same activity was likely to bulge up somewhere else at the price of serious disruption of service and increased costs at another level.

Certainly within the confines of primary stage conditions, there can be many innovations to improve efficiency. The adaptation of self-service, vending machines, and mail-order service in the USSR was undertaken because of a desire for increased productivity—the same stimulus that led to the introduction of these activities in the West. Not only do such innovations result in a need for fewer salesclerks, but in the case of mail-order service, the number of remote and specialized outlets can be reduced.

Despite certain complications, the over-all effect of

self-service, vending machines, and mail-order service has been to improve the service and reduce the cost of performing the basic primary stage functions of retailing and wholesaling. Moreover, from a Marxist point of view, such innovations involve no ideological heresy. Marx certainly would have been gratified to see the efficiency of the middleman increased and his costs of operation reduced as a result of these particular improvements. It seems unlikely, however, that he would have been quite as pleased at the developments to be discussed next.

The Secondary Stage. We now turn to a fascinating chapter in Soviet economic history—the development of the secondary stage of marketing. As was mentioned earlier, the secondary stage is characterized by a fundamental change in supply-and-demand relationships. Instead of long queues and perennial shortages, nationwide buyer's markets develop. Furthermore, large numbers of consumers begin to have surplus, or discretionary, income at their disposal.

While a prerequisite of the secondary stage is the existence of a buyer's market, this is not the only condition. Local buyer's markets may, in fact, exist in the primary stage. For instance, because of faulty allocation of goods, Irkutsk in Siberia may receive a winter shipment of bathing suits, creating a buyer's market there, even though the over-all demand for bathing suits is far from satisfied in the Crimea or the rest of the country. For the purposes of this study, secondary stage conditions are said to exist when nationwide supplies of various goods, especially durables, begin to exceed demand at the existing price. The effects can be observed even though this may hold only for certain categories of goods. To illustrate again, whereas reshipping the goods from Irkutsk may completely settle the bathing suit problem in the primary stage, reshipping alone is not the solution in the secondary stage. If the goods are to be sold, other measures must be taken.

Similarly, it is not enough that nationwide buyer's markets exist. Buyer's markets have existed in all stages of economic development. It is also necessary that discretionary income be at the disposal of a large number of consumers. Moreover, the existence of this surplus income must not be the result of a shortage of goods or a seller's market. Instead, because of improvements in their standard of living, consumers find that they need spend only a part of their current incomes in order to live. As general living conditions are raised far enough above subsistence, portions of current income can be set aside for disposal or major purchases at a later date.

Therefore, the secondary stage must be characterized by a nationwide buyer's market *and* the existence of discretionary income. The producer finds himself under pressure to please and attract customers with the knowledge that the customer has the means at his disposal to make a purchase.

Another problem from the distributor's point of view is that it is no longer simply a question of calculating demand for such inelastic items as bread and potatoes. Demand for elastic goods like appliances and stylistic clothing must be anticipated. In order to maintain inventories at their previous low levels, it is necessary to estimate where, when, and what the consumer will buy. As the selection and variety of goods grow, so does the task of calculating and allocating demand for these products. When a society reaches a certain state of affluence, many activities of large numbers of its consumers are likely to be unpredictable.

As a result of such conditions, the middleman becomes much more important and the scope of his functions is enlarged. To balance production and consumption, it is no longer enough that retailers confine their activities to maintaining shops accessible to the consumer, nor is it enough that the other intermediaries store and reassemble goods. To cope with a consumer who has become quite fickle, new forms of distribution activity are required. Market research is now necessary to ascertain what the consumer wants, and merchandising is needed to convince the consumer and make it easy for him to buy.

How does all of this relate to the Soviet Union, the land of the planned economy and the seven-year plan, where "the nature of Soviet trade results in a planned balance between production and consumption" (Gogol', 1958, p. 17)? No one who has ever seen the meager apartment of an upper-income or middle-class Russian or the inside of a Soviet department store with its long lines and poorly fashioned goods would even suggest that the Russians have reached the advanced phases of the secondary stage of marketing development that characterizes marketing in the Western world. None the less, there are definite signs that the Russians are now experiencing the problems common to the more "affluent" stage.

As an indication of the overproduction of certain items, there are frequent complaints in the press about excessive inventory formation and accumulation of goods.* For some articles like watches, there seems to be a surplus at all price

---

* For examples, see *Ekonomicheskaia Gazeta,* Dec. 25, 1961, p. 32; *Sovetskaia Torgovlia,* Mar. 28, 1957, p. 2, Aug. 19, 1959, p. 2; *Sovetskaia Moldavia,* Feb. 1, 1958, p. 2. See also the remarkable article, "Nekhodovye Tovary I Ikh Utsenka," by M. Zak, *Sovetskaia Torgovlia,* Oct., 1960, p. 11.

ranges. Watches are now in such abundance that almost nobody buys them from the mail-order service any more, even though they were once a major component of mail-order sales volume. Khrushchev gave them away in Pittsburgh, and the Russians sell them for $9.00 in Cuba. For the most part, however, Soviet affluence extends only to the more expensive models of such products as television sets, radios, bicycles, hunting equipment, and cameras.

Since only a few upper-income families in the Soviet Union can afford, say, the combination television, radio, and phonograph set that costs $1,400 or a $220 camera, once these families have made their purchases, something must be done to widen the market. The solution thus far seems to have been something equivalent to a sales promotion campaign. With essentially all the familiar capitalist trappings, there have been price reductions, product differentiation, advertising, installment sales, and trade fairs.

PRICE REDUCTIONS. The easiest way to solve the problems of the secondary stage is to reduce prices. While there were annual price reductions for large numbers of goods from 1947 to 1954, these moves were principally aimed at providing an improved standard of living. The alternative was to allow wage increases. Throughout most of this period there were still great shortages of almost all categories of goods.

After 1954, however, the ritual of widespread annual price reductions ceased. The markdowns made thereafter covered only a carefully selected list of goods—significantly, goods in excessive supply. For the most part, the same items were selected each year. Beginning in August, 1956, there were consecutive price reductions in April, 1957, January, 1958, July, 1959, and March, 1960, of the expensive models of television sets, cameras, radios, and watches. As explained by Mikoyan, "The television sets were good, but were being reluctantly purchased. These were accumulating in the stores. The Minister of Trade, instead of demanding a decrease in the television set production plan, created a supplemental demand for them by means of a price reduction" (*Kommunist*, March 12, 1958, p. 2). This opened up a new and broader market.

While this may be an important means of solving the dilemmas of the secondary stage, selective price reductions, together with a general disregard for the principles of the labor theory of value, tend to create a cleavage between Soviet pricing practice and Marxist pricing theory.

ADVERTISING. Advertising is another solution for the problems of the secondary stage. While it is impossible to compare Soviet advertising with the scale and scope of advertising in the United States, the Russians use advertising for much the same purpose. For example, when a large shipment of herring suddenly arrived, Soviet trade officials were criticized for not advertising in order to broaden the market. It was felt that this would have prevented the spoilage that eventually resulted.

Of the secondary stage symptoms in the Soviet Union, advertising is one of the most interesting. In recent years the range of advertising activities has grown from newspaper advertisements and occasional billboard displays to include radio and television commercials, window display contests, All-Socialist Advertising Conferences, special courses in advertising technique, and finally the creation of official advertising agencies in the republics as described in Chapter 2. Advertising copy is prepared, display ideas suggested, and outdoor advertising coordinated—all for a fee, of course.

While much of the advertising is still informational in

nature, more and more of it is becoming competitive. To illustrate, often in the same paper the consumer is urged through advertisements to visit GUM and TsUM, Moscow's two leading department stores, because each one insists that it offers "the best in service." The Moscow consumer is further torn between Fish Shop No. 2 and Fish Shop No. 10, because both advertise that they offer the freshest fish. Competing claims can also be seen now in advertisements appearing for different brands of radios and television sets.

What accounts for this relatively sudden acceleration of advertising activity? The most obvious answer is the appearance of buyer's market conditions and the availability of discretionary income—the conditions of our secondary stage. T. Stepaniants, the director of *Torgreklama,* the advertising agency of the Russian Republic, stated in a personal interview:

> Because of increased production, the store managers now recognize that it is necessary to show the advantages of the many new goods that are being offered for sale. The store managers themselves were creating their own small advertising units to do this work, and we decided to coordinate and centralize their activities.

While Stepaniants acknowledged that there had been some uneasiness about accommodating his organization to the Marxist tradition, he felt that such attitudes had changed as store directors faced up to the problems of selling their merchandise and reducing their inventories.

PRODUCT DIFFERENTIATION. Where there is advertising, there is likely to be product differentiation, but product differentiation has found its way into the USSR for other reasons as well. One of these is quality maintenance. By differentiating one factory's products from another, the

Russian authorities have found that they can take effective administrative action in the event of faulty production, since they can immediately determine which factory is responsible. Further, some of the costs of administration may be reduced as a result of the realization by the factory that poor quality will be easily discovered. The savings in administrative expense may more than offset the wastes connected with production inefficiency and the costs of advertising.

Much the same argument applies in connection with off-setting the costs of distribution. Russian marketing officials have suggested that, within limits, the added expenses resulting from advertising and product differentiation make possible somewhat larger savings in the operation of a self-service system. If the efficiencies of self-service are to be realized, the record shows, advertising and product differentiation seem to be essential.

INSTALLMENT CREDIT. While advertising and product differentiation may play an important role in the primary and secondary stages of growth, the use of installment credit would appear to be restricted largely to the latter stage. Although certain areas in the Soviet Union have been experimenting with consumer credit since 1958, the official announcement that it was to be introduced throughout the Soviet Union came in August, 1959. The excited tone of the official newspaper announcement is in itself fascinating: "This department store sells on installment. . . . Such an advertisement will soon be seen in many city store windows. For sale on credit! How magnificent!" (*Sovet-skaia Rossiia,* Aug. 16, 1959, p. 4).

With 25 per cent down and six months to pay at a 1–2 per cent interest rate, the consumer will be able to buy any camera costing more than $40, bicycles, motorcycles, watches, television sets, and radios. For the first time young married couples will be able to purchase durable goods that otherwise they would be unable to afford for several years. What lies behind this change? The most obvious answer is that the government wanted to make life more comfortable for those without immediate funds, but the demand-and-supply conditions of the limited assortment of goods to be sold on credit seem to indicate that an equally important motive for the revolutionary innovation was the need to increase the sale of certain slow-moving items. The fact that large numbers of consumers' goods all in short supply were not to be sold on installment credit reinforces this theory.

DECENTRALIZATION. There is yet one other marketing technique used by the Russians to cope with the effects of the secondary stage. As the customer finds he has the chance to select not just a shirt but a shirt with a particular color, collar style, sleeve, and material, the store manager finds that with so many variables it is increasingly difficult to forecast the demand. Recently, intermediary or middlemen offices (*Posrednicheskie Kontory*) have been created at the wholesale level to help solve this aspect of the problem. In order to recirculate surplus stocks of retail and wholesale trade organizations, these middlemen offices issue bulletins and descriptions of stocks and wants. Moreover, they organize biannual and special trade fairs for the traditional purpose of bringing buyers and sellers together.

It is not only surplus stocks that are sold and resold. More and more, factory products enter the channels of distribution directly through trade fairs. With their ideal of the planned economic order, the Communists have long scorned the trade fairs of Nizhni Novgorod and Kiev that characterized the Czarist era. Yet promotions similar in nature are now being officially sponsored, and sales volume at one such fair amounted to more than 10 billion rubles. As the variety and assortment of goods increases, it becomes more and more difficult to plan their distribution in a centralized manner.

The Russians have apparently decided, therefore, to further the decentralization of the consumers' goods distribution system. While the abolition of the all-Union Ministry of Trade is one reflection of this, perhaps the most extreme step has been the revival of the decentralized allocation mechanism, the trade fair.

There is of course another (nonmarketing) solution to the problem: the production plan can be altered. By continually calling for increases in yearly production, the planners may be causing their own problems. (The reduction of watch, camera, and bicycle production since 1959 seems to be a recognition of this.) None the less, while the decision has been made, secondary stage marketing conditions do seem to be inevitable. Furthermore, secondary stage marketing conditions may develop, at least in the short run, regardless of the intentions of the planners, because of the consumer's fickleness about style or because of production inflexibility. D. D. Korolev, the Assistant Minister of Trade of the RSFSR, during a recent visit to Boston acknowledged that radios, cameras, and rifles were being overproduced in the Soviet Union. The radio problem was solved partially by a price reduction and partially by converting some of the radio factories to the production of television sets. Unfortunately, the camera and rifle glut has not been fully alleviated. Price reductions, advertising, and installment credit helped, but since it apparently is more difficult to convert camera and rifle factories, Korolev indirectly suggested that a more logical solution would be to export the surplus.

CONCLUSION

What is the significance of all this? Many Westerners will draw a sigh of relief, say "I told you so," and mumble to themselves, "I knew it had to happen; aren't the Russians human?"

Perhaps this is the real explanation. Russian consumers are human, which means that, if given the opportunity, they are unpredictable. The minute that they are supplied with something more than their basic needs and are allowed to exercise a degree of choice, it becomes hard to anticipate their actions. As mentioned in Chapter 3, it is no longer sufficient to predict the number of Russians who will want a size 15 collar and a size 33 sleeve; it is necessary to plan how many of these people will want blue, white, or gray with plain, tabbed, or button-down collars and in cotton, oxford, or nylon cloth—not to mention sleeve or style variations. Naturally, it is impossible to do this on a centralized basis without making serious mistakes. Even if the decision-making is decentralized, there will be mistakes, that, once the goods are produced, necessitate price reductions, advertising, product differentiation, and credit. This argument in no way reflects on whether or not centralized planning is effective with heavy industrial goods. Knowing the technological input coefficient in steel production, the planners may be able to predict accurately how much coal, iron ore, and limestone will be needed; but at the consumers' goods level the problems are quite different.

As for the marketing functions themselves, it seems clear that there are certain basic operations that must be performed regardless of the stage of marketing development. Whether in India or in a pure Marxist state, retailing and certain wholesaling activities must be carried out even in the early years. At the second stage of marketing development, a whole new range of activities connected with market research and merchandising becomes important and vital even though such activities lead to an increase in the costs of distribution. While it is not to be denied that many of these new activities are frequently too wide in scope and wasteful, they nevertheless perform an important function at a certain level of economic development. Consequently, the ideal marketing system of the social critic seems farther away than ever. Instead of the elimination of duplication (one milk company delivering milk on a street instead of several), the secondary stage usually means that more costly and complex methods of merchandising and market research are needed (advertising and reducing the prices of unsalable goods).

Because of chronic shortages of goods in the past (and in some instances, at present), the Russians have never had to face these facts until recent years. Whatever Russian industry produced was sold. They could insist that any undue activity by a middleman inevitably was a sign of inefficiency and waste and was a phenomenon peculiar to capitalism. But the Soviet standard of living has been gradually improving. Now that the first faint signs of the secondary stage of marketing development have started to appear, the Russian system of distribution of consumers' goods has begun to resemble the Western system more and more. In the future, as it becomes increasingly difficult to make comprehensive consumption and distribution plans, it seems logical to expect an even greater reliance on the traditional capitalist marketing practices, regardless of the teachings of Marx.

Appendix

HISTORICAL

BACKGROUND

FORTUNATELY there have been at least three competent historical descriptions of Soviet trade covering the period up to 1950 (Hubbard, 1938; Chossudousky, June, 1941, Nov., 1941; Ware, July, 1950, Oct., 1950). Since detailed discussion is available to the reader in English, it will only be necessary here to describe the more significant trends.

At an early date after the revolution, a new type of cooperative society was formed to supply the needs of the population. Despite the fact that membership was compulsory, the organization failed for the simple reason that the chaos that followed in the wake of the revolution left little semblance of order or organization in domestic distribution. In the following NEP period, conditions improved and sales by cooperative organizations increased significantly. (See Table 1.) Private trade was permitted, if not encouraged, until the early 1930's when the state felt itself strong enough to eliminate it. Actually, private trade did continue, but under the pseudonym of *kolkhoz* market trade.

The inauguration of the five-year plans and the collectivization of agriculture once again disrupted the normal distribution channels that had been reconstructed during the NEP period. The solution in this instance was rationing. However, the full impact of rationing was often averted by recourse to the use of special stores selling to privileged customers or other stores selling to all customers, but at prices far above the official rates.

By the time rationing was abolished in 1936, the basic pattern of retail trade had been established. Cooperative stores, at one time the largest retail network, were confined to rural areas, and government stores were permitted an operating monopoly in urban areas. This pattern persisted until the outbreak of war in 1941, when rationing and the privileged-store system of shopping was reintroduced. It was as if conditions existing during the last crisis period of the early 1930's had been duplicated in exact detail. It was even decided to allow cooperative stores in the cities again.

The war years were extremely difficult. Despite all the attempts to provide new trading methods, the *kolkhoz* market often became the only source of food. In 1945, 51 per cent of total food sales volume was transacted in *kolkhoz* markets. Because of heavily inflated prices, the absolute volume of goods sold was much smaller, but other outlets often had no supplies at all.

The currency reform of 1947 brought an end to rationing and a return to normalcy, albeit an austere form of it. The basic structure of the retail network was converted to its prewar pattern when the consumer cooperatives were again returned to the countryside. More important for the people, however, was a series of yearly price reductions and an increasing sales volume that combined to bring about a gradual improvement in the standard of living. The fluctuations of trade and the shifts in prominence between various retail outlets can be traced in the sales statistics given in Table 1.

The history of changes at the wholesale and administrative levels follows closely the changes at the retail level. As Figure 7 indicates, there were many changes at the upper echelons. The evolution of the present wholesaling system took place in the twenties and thirties as the state gradually asserted itself and attained more and more control over the distribution sections. The state replaced the private enterprises, but not the essential functions. It was discovered that the basic operations could be assigned to different organizations, but they had to be performed none the less.

One interesting instance of this is cited by Hubbard. An attempt was made to abolish certain wholesaling functions of the consumer societies. Intermediary cooperative wholesale depots were abolished, and it was reasoned that the *sbyt* organizations of industry could deliver the goods directly to the retail outlet, thereby eliminating an unnecessary and expensive distribution operation. Unfortunately, it was not so simple:

> the managers of the rural cooperative societies were generally ignorant of which manufacturing enterprises were in a position to supply their requirements, and in any case it was a greater tax on their intelligence to write out

Figure 7—Evolution of Central Organization for Domestic Trade

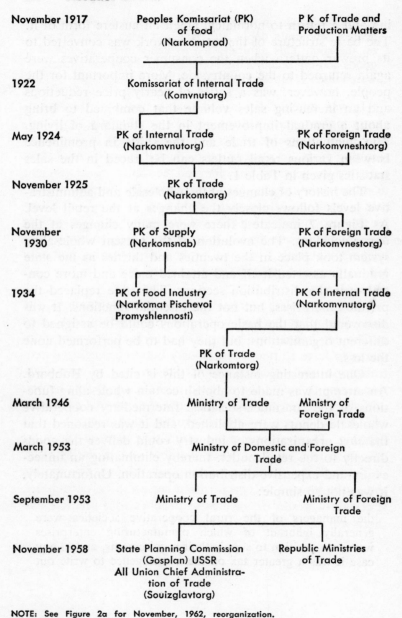

November 1917 — Peoples Komissariat (PK) of food (Narkomprod) — P K of Trade and Production Matters

1922 — Komissariat of Internal Trade (Komvnutorg)

May 1924 — PK of Internal Trade (Narkomvnutorg) — PK of Foreign Trade (Narkomvneshtorg)

November 1925 — PK of Trade (Narkomtorg)

November 1930 — PK of Supply (Narkomsnab) — PK of Foreign Trade (Narkomvnestorg)

1934 — PK of Food Industry (Narkomat Pischevoi Promyshlennosti) — PK of Internal Trade (Narkomvnutorg)

PK of Trade (Narkomtorg)

March 1946 — Ministry of Trade — Ministry of Foreign Trade

March 1953 — Ministry of Domestic and Foreign Trade

September 1953 — Ministry of Trade — Ministry of Foreign Trade

November 1958 — State Planning Commission (Gosplan) USSR All Union Chief Administration of Trade (Souizglavtorg) — Republic Ministries of Trade

NOTE: See Figure 2a for November, 1962, reorganization.

orders for goods on distant enterprises than to go to their nearest wholesale depot and pick out what they wanted on the spot. This naturally led to delay in the receipt of goods and the accumulation of stocks in the manufacturers' warehouses (Hubbard, 1938, p. 41).

It was quickly discovered that because of the significantly higher transportation costs of sending small, special, broken-lot shipments of goods and the delays in shipments resulting from an already overcrowded transportation system, it was actually cheaper and certainly more efficient to reintroduce intermediary and seemingly parasitic wholesale operations. All the state could hope to do was to transfer the responsibility for the performance of the wholesaling functions from one agency to another. The increased bookkeeping resulting from the broken-lot ordering not only led to immeasurably poorer services but it in no way reduced costs.

Amid countless reorganizations and redesignations, the basic administrative and wholesale organizations described in Chapter 2 came into being. The organizational pendulum seems to have shifted continuously between increased centralization and decentralization. The apogee of centralization seems to have been reached in the early 1950's before, and shortly after, Stalin's death; but even in that confusing era, a movement toward decentralization seemed to be forming. The resulting trend ultimately reached the stage described in Chapter 2 when the abolition of the Ministry of Trade of the USSR was announced. While at this writing the move toward decentralization seems to be continuing, it certainly would be an unwise prophet who predicts that there will never be any movement in the opposite direction.

BIBLIOGRAPHY

BOOKS AND ARTICLES

Abaturov, A. I. *Isderzhki Obrashcheniia v Roznichnoi Torgovle i Osnovnye Puti ikh Snizneniia.* Moscow: Gostorgizdat, 1956.

Abutkova, G. V. *Ob Izuchenii Kon'iunktury Sovetskoi Torgovli.* Moscow: Gostorgizdat, 1949.

————. *Ob Izuchenii Kon'iunktury Sovetskoi Torgovli.* Moscow: Gostorgizdat, 1954.

Alderson, Wroe, and Sessions, Roger E. *Cost and Profit Outlook,* Vol. VIII, No. 7, July, 1955.

Amunov, S. "Zadachi Rabotnikov Sovetskoi Torgovli v Udovletvorenii Sprosa Potrebitelei," *Kommunist Tadzhikstana,* December 17, 1958.

Babushkin, V. I. *Spravochnik Nalogovogo Rabotnika.* Moscow: Gosfinizdat, 1958.

Bakanov, M. I. *Bor'ba za Ekonomichnost' Tovarnogo Obrashcheniia v SSSR.* Moscow: Gostorgizdat, 1958.

————. *Izderzhki Tovarnogo Obrashcheniia v SSSR.* Moscow: Gostorgizdat, 1959.

————. "K Ekonomicheskoi Kharakteristike Izderzhek Tovarnogo Obrashcheniia v *SSSR," Sovetskaia Torgovlia,* April, 1957.

Barger, Harold. *Distribution's Place in the American Economy since 1869.* Princeton, N.J.: Princeton University Press, 1955.

Bergson, Abram. *Soviet National Income and Product in 1937.* New York: Columbia University Press, 1953.

Berliner, Joseph. *Factory and Manager in the USSR.* Cambridge, Mass.: Harvard University Press, 1957.

Bespalov, M. "Voprosy Uluchsheniia Optovoi Torgovli," *Sovetskaia Torgovlia,* March, 1960.

Birman, A. M. *Finansy Otraslei Narodnogo Khoziaistva SSSR,* Vol. II. Moscow: Gosfinizdat, 1957.

Bukh, E. M. *Torgovlia pri Sotsializme.* Moscow: Sovetskaia Nauka, 1959.

Bukhanevich, B., and Sonin, M. "Mezhraionnom Regulirovanii Zarabotnoi Platy v SSSR," *Voprosy Ekonomiki,* January, 1957.

Campbell, Robert W. "A Comparison of Soviet and American Investory-Output Ratios," *American Economic Review,* September, 1958.

Chamberlin, Edward H. *The Theory of Monopolistic Competition* (6th ed.). Cambridge, Mass.: Harvard University Press, 1950.

Chossudousky, E. M. "Derationing in the USSR," *Review of Economic Studies,* November, 1941 [a].

————. "Rationing in the USSR," *ibid.,* June, 1941 [b].

Dadugin, A. P., and Fedorov, P. N. *Organizatsiia Kolkhoznoi Rynochnoi Torgovli.* Moscow, Gostorgizdat, 1957.

Dadugin, A. P., and Ronin, L. Kh. *Spravochnik Direktora Kolkhoznoi Rynka*. Moscow: Gostorgizdat, 1957.

Davydov, V., and Kuprienko, A. "Uprostit' Finansovoe Planirovanie v Torgakh Trestakh Stolovykh," *Sovetskaia Torgovlia*, July, 1961.

Davydov, V. I., and Uspenskii, E. I. *Mekhanizatsiia Ucheta v Torgovle*. Moscow: Gostorgizdat, 1957.

D'iachenko, N. A. *Nalogovaia Bukhralteriia* (2nd rev. ed.). Moscow: Gosfinizdat, 1955.

Druzhinin, N. K. *Matematiko-Statisticheskie Metody Analiza Ekspertimental'nykh Dannykh v Tovarovedenii*. Moscow: Gostorgizdat, 1959.

England, Wilbur B. *Operating Results of Food Chains in 1960*. Boston: Harvard University Graduate School of Business Administration, Bureau of Business Research, Bulletin, No. 162, September, 1961.

Fedorov, P. N. *Organizatsionnoe Postroenie Sovetskaia Torgovli*. Moscow: Gostorgizdat, 1957.

Fefilov, A. I. *Roznichnaia Torgovlia v SSSR*. Moscow: Gostorgizdat, 1957.

Gatovskii, I. M. (ed.). *Izderzhki Obrashcheniia v SSSR i Puti ikh Snizheniia*. Moscow: Akademiia Nauk, Gospolitizdat, 1955.

Genkin, D. M., and Fialkov, M. A. (eds.). *Pravovoe Regulirovanie Gosudarstvennoi Torgovlie SSSR*. Moscow: Gostorgizdat, 1957.

Gerasimov, V. A. *Vitrinnoe Okno*. Moscow: Gostorgizdat, 1958.

Gogol', B. I. (ed.). *40 Let Sovetskoi Torgovli*. Moscow: Gostorgizdat, 1957.

————. *Ekonomika Sovetskoi Torgovli.* Moscow: Gospolitizdat, 1958.

————. *Ibid.,* 1959.

————. *Ibid.,* 1960.

Goldman, Marshall I. "Commission Trade and the Kolkhoz Market," *Soviet Studies,* October, 1958.

————. "Product Differentiation and Advertising: Some Lessons from Soviet Experience," *The Journal of Political Economy,* August, 1960.

————. "The Soviet Standard of Living and Ours," *Foreign Affairs,* July, 1960.

Gringauz, K. L., and Sablina, T. N. *Izuchenie Pokupatel'-skogo Sprosa na Tkani.* Moscow: Gostorgizdat, 1957.

Guz, R. Z. *Izuchenie Pokupatel'skogo Sprosa i ego Udovletvorenie* (2nd ed.). Moscow: Gostorgizdat, 1958.

Guzman, A. A., Zaitsev, V. A., Kurkin, S. L., Pronichkina, L. P., and Smirnov, V. B. *Panel'nye Torgovye Avtomaty dlia Predpriiatii Obshchestvennogo Pitaniia.* Moscow: Gostorgizdat, 1958.

Holzman, Franklyn. "Soviet Inflationary Pressures, 1928-57; Causes and Cures," *Quarterly Journal of Economics,* May, 1960.

————. *Soviet Taxation.* Cambridge, Mass.: Harvard University Press, 1955.

Hubbard, Leonard E. *Soviet Trade and Distribution.* London: Macmillan & Co. Ltd., 1938.

Ikonnikov, V. V. *Kredit v Sotsialisticheskom Obshchestve.* Moscow: Gosfinizdat, 1959.

Isaacson, H. Lawrence. *Operating Results of Department and Specialty Stores in 1960.* Boston: Harvard University Graduate School of Business Administration, Bureau of Business Research, Bulletin, No. 161, August, 1961.

Itin, M. A., and Sokolov, V. G. *Planirovanie Roznichnogo Tovarooborota i Tovarnykh Fondov.* Moscow: Gostorgizdat, 1954.

Itin, M. A. *Raschety Pokupatel'nykh Fondov Naselenia.* Moscow: Gostorgizdat, 1951.

Jasny, Naum. *The Soviet 1956 Statistical Handbook: A Commentary.* East Lansing: The Michigan State University Press, 1957.

Kamenev, V. G. *G.U.M.* Moscow: Gostorgizdat, 1956.

Kaplan, A. I. *Oborotnye Sredstva Sovetskoi Torgovle.* Moscow: Gostorgizdat, 1959.

Kaplan, Norman, and Wainstein, Eleanor. *A Comparison of Soviet and American Retail Prices in 1950.* Santa Monica, Calif.: RAND, 1957 [a].

———— and ————. *An Addendum to Previous USSR-US Retail Price Comparisons.* Santa Monica, Calif.: RAND, 1957 [b].

Katal'nikov, I. F. *Statistika Sovetskoi Torgovli.* Moscow: Gostorgizdat, 1957.

Khrekin, I. M. *Izuchenie Sprosa v. Torgovle.* Moscow: Gostorgizdat, 1957.

————. *Pokupatel'naia Sposobnost' Naseleniia i Tovarooborot.* Moscow: Gostorgizdat, 1958.

————. "Razvitie Tovarooborota v 1958 r.," *Sovetskaia Torgovlia,* January, 1959.

Khrekin, I., and Smoktii, D. "Sovershenstvovat' Statistiki Torgovli," *Sovetskaia Torgovlia,* May, 1956.

Kolosovskii, S. Ia., and Rozenblium, Iu. A. *Nolog s Oborota.* Khar'kov: Izdatel'stvo Khar'kovskogo Universiteta, 1958.

Kondrashov, D. C. *Tsenoobrazovanie v Promyshlennosti SSSR.* Moscow: Gosfinizdat, 1956.

————. "Tsenoobrazovanie Vazhnyi Faktor Razvitiia Narodnogo Khoziaistva i Ukrepleniia Denezhnogo Obrashcheniia," *Dengy i Kredit,* No. 9, 1958.

Korzhenevskii, I. "Opredelenie Sprosa Naseleniia na Otdel'nye Tovary," *Sovetskaia Torgovlia,* March, 1959.

Kovylin, V. A. *Nalog s Oborota po Promyshlennym Tovaram.* Moscow: Gosfinizdat, 1958.

Kozlov, G. A., and Pervushin, S. P. (eds.). *Kratkii Ekonomicheskii Slovar'.* Moscow: Gospolitizdat, 1958.

Kozlov, V. V. *50 Let Instituta G. V. Plekhanova.* Moscow: Gostorgizdat, 1957.

Kronrod, Ia. A. (ed.). *Zakon Stoimosti i Ego Ispol'zovanie v Narodnom Khoziaistve SSSR.* Moscow: Gospolitizdat, 1959.

Kulikov, A. "O Nekotorykh Voprosakh Ispol'zovaniia Zakono Stoimosti i Tsenoobrazovanii v SSSR," *Voprosy Ekonomiki,* No. 8, 1958.

Kulikov, A. G., and Smotrina, N. A. *Tseny na Predmety Potrebleniia v SSSR,* Vol. V. Moscow: Gostorgizdat, 1959.

Kurnin, D. N. *Posylochnaia Torgovlia za Rubezhom.* Moscow: Gostorgizdat, 1956.

Lartsev, F. F. *Torgovlia Pri Sotsializme.* Moscow: Izdatel'stvo VPSh i AON pri TsK KPSS, 1959.

Lavrov, V. V. (ed.). *Finansirovanie Otraslei Narodnogo Khoziaistva.* Moscow: Gosfinizdat, 1956.

Leningrad Kratkii Spravochnik. Leningrad: Lenizdat, 1957.

Levine, Herbert S. "Centralized Planning of Supply in Soviet Industry," *Comparisons of the United States and Soviet Economies,* Part I, Subcommittee on Economic Statistics of the Joint Economic Committee. Washington, D.C.: Government Printing Office, 1959.

Lifits, M. M. (ed.). *Ekonomika Sovetskoi Torgovli.* Moscow: Gostorgizdat, 1950.

————. *Ibid.,* 1955.

————. *Optovaia Torgovlia v SSSR.* Moscow: Gostorgizdat, 1956.

————. *Sovetskaia Torgovlia i ee Rol' v Ekonomicheskoi Zhizni Strany.* Moscow: Gospolitizdat, 1951.

————. *Sovetskaia Torgovlia Vazhnoe Sredstvo Povysheniia Blagosostoianiia Trudiashchikhsia.* Moscow: Znanie, 1953.

————. *Torgovo-Finansovyi Plan Torga.* Moscow: Gostorgizdat, 1948.

Lifits, M. M. "Nekotorye Voprosy Tovarnogo Obrashcheniia v SSSR na Sovremennom Etape," *Voprosy Ekonomiki,* November, 1959.

Lisitsian, N. *Kreditovanie Gosudarstvennoi Roznichnoi Torgovli v SSSR.* Moscow: Gosfinizdat, 1957.

Lomovatskii, E. G., and Gromova, G. M. *Upravlenie Gosudarstvennoi Vnutrennei Torgovlei v SSSR.* Moscow: Gosiurizdat, 1957.

Lopatkin, V. "Sovetskaia Torgovlia—Forma Raspedeleniia Predmetov Potrebleniia," *Voprosy Ekonomiki,* March, 1954.

McNair, Malcolm P. *Operating Results of Department and*

Specialty Stores in 1958. Boston: Harvard University Graduate School of Business Administration, Bureau of Business Research Bulletin, No. 155, 1959.

Makarov, A. D. *Finansirovanie i Kreditovanie Sovetskoi Torgovli.* Moscow: Gostorgizdat, 1955.

―――. *Finansy Sovetskoi Torgovli.* Moscow: Gostorgizdat, 1956.

Makarova, M. *Sovetskaia Torgovlia i Narodnoe Potreblenia.* Moscow: Gospolitizdat, 1954.

―――. *O Tovarnom Proizvodstve i Zakone Stoimosti pri Sotsializme.* Moscow: Gospolitizdat, 1958.

Marx, Karl. *Capital,* Vol. II. Chicago: Charles Kerr, 1925.

Mekhanizatsiia Ucheta v Sovetskoi Torgovle-Sbornik Statei. Moscow: Gostorgizdat, 1957.

Merton, Robert K. *Social Theory and Social Structure.* New York: The Free Press of Glencoe, 1951.

Mezhiborskaia, S., and Mosikovich, E. "Novoe v Kreditovanii Torgovli," *Den'gi i Kredit,* January, 1956.

Mikoyan, A. I. *Measures for the Further Expansion of Trade and for Improving the Organization of State, Cooperative and Collective Farm Trade.* Moscow: Foreign Language Publishing House, 1954.

―――. "Nekotorye Voprosy Torgovli," *Sovetskaia Torgovlia,* May, 1958.

Ministerstvo Torgovli RSFSR, Posyltorg. *Tovary Pochtoi Katalog.* Moscow, 1958–59.

―――. *Tovary Pochtoi—Preiskurant.* Moscow, 1959.

Mochalov, B. "Razvitie Sovetskii Torgovli," *Vestnik Moskovskogo Universiteta,* No. 8, 1958.

Montias, J. M. "Planning with Material Balances in Soviet Type Economies," *American Economic Review,* December, 1959.

Moskovskaia Gorodskaia Spravochno–Informatsionnaia

Kontora. "Mosgorspravka," *Moskva Kratkaia Adresno —Spravochnaia Kniga*. Moscow, 1956.
————. *Ibid.*, 1958.

Nauchno-Issledovatel'skii Institut Torgovli i Obshchestvennogo Pitaniia Ministerstva Torgovli SSSR. *Normy Estestvennoi Ubuli Prodovol'stvennykh Tovarov*. Moscow: Gostorgizdat, 1958.

Nefedov, G. "Nekotorye Storony Raboty Apparata Ministerstva," *Izvestiia*, No. 7, July, 1958.

Nemchinov, V. S. *Uchenye Zapiski Po Statistike*, Vol. I. Moscow: Izdatel'stvo Akademii Nauk SSSR, 1955.

Oblovatskii, F. Ia. *Ekonomika i Planirovanie Sovetskoi Torgovli*. Moscow: Gostorgizdat, 1949.

Parkinson, C. Northcote. *Parkinson's Law*. Boston: Houghton Mifflin, 1957.

Pavlov, D. V. *Razvitie Sovetskoi Torgovli v Poslevoennye Gody*. Moscow: Izdatel'stvo, V. P. Sh. i A. O. N. pri TsKKPSS, 1958.

Phillips, Charles F., and Duncan, Delbert J. *Marketing Principles and Methods*. Homewood, Ill.: Richard D. Irwin, 1956.

Pisarev, I. Iu. (ed.). *Metodologicheskie Voprosy Izucheniia Urovnia Zhizni Trudiashchikhsia*. Moscow: Sotsekgiz, 1959.

Riauzov, N. N., and Pisarev, I. Iu. *Kurs Torgovoi Statistiki*. Moscow: Soiuzorguchet, 1938.

Riauzov, N. N., and Tenebaum, M. V. *Torgovo Kooperativnaia Statistika*. Moscow: Gostorgizdat, 1939.

Riauzov, N. N., and Titel'baum, N. P. *Kurs Torgovoi Statiski.* Moscow: Gosplanizdat, 1947.

Rostovskii na Donu. *Planirovanie Mestnogo Khoziaistva i Kul'turnogo Stroitel'stva Administrativnogo Raiona.* Moscow: Gospolitizdat, 1957.

Rubinshtein, Ia. *Ocherki Razvitiia Sovetskogo Kredita.* Moscow: Gosfinizdat, 1958.

Sadov, V. I. *Moskovsko-Leninskii Univermag.* Moscow: Gostorgizdat, 1958.

Sapel'nikov, Ia. "Chto Pokazal Edinovremmennyi Uchet Tovarnykh Zapasov," *Sovetskaia Torgovlia,* December, 1959.

Sapel'nikiv, Ia., Shnirlin, and Levin, A. "Neosushchestvimye Predlozheniia," *Sovetskaia Torgovlia,* July, 1959.

Serebriakov, S. V. *Organizatsiia Tsentralizovannoi Dostavki Torvarov.* Moscow: Gostorgizdat, 1958.

————. *Organizatsiia i Tekhniki Sovetskoi Torgovli.* Moscow: Gostorgizdat, 1949.

————. *Ibid.,* 1956.

Serebrennikov, I. "Nekotorye Voprosy Organizatsii Optovoi Torgovli," *Sovetskaia Torgovlia,* October, 1960.

Shkrebel', M. "Iz Opyta Obsledovaniia Biudzhetov Kolkhoznikov," *Vestnik Statistiki,* No. 1, 1957.

Skovoroda, K. "Zadachi Dal'neishego Uluchsheniia Torgovogo Obsluzhivaniia Naselennia," *Planovoe Khoziaistvo,* February, 1960.

Skvortsov, L. "Nekotorye Voprosy Planirovaniia Tsen na Predmety Narodnogo Potrebleniia," *Voprosy Ekonomiki,* June, 1958.

————. "Nekotorye Zadachi Regulirovaniia Roznichnikh Tsen," *Voprosy Ekonomiki,* April, 1957.

Smirnov, A. I. (ed.). *Restorannaia Promyshlennost' S Sh A*. Moscow: Gostorgizdat, 1957.

Sobolev, A. I. *Torgovlia v Leningrade*. Moscow: Gostorgizdat, 1958.

Sokolov, V., and Nazarov, R. *Sovetskaia Torgovlia v Poslevoennyi Period*. Moscow: Gospolitizdat, 1954.

Spasskii, A. "Nuzhen li Predvaritel'nyi Aktsept?" *Den'gi i Kredit*, December, 1956.

SSSR Kak On Est'. Moscow: Gospolitizdat, 1959.

Starozum, G. *Puti Snizheniia Izderzhek v Obshchestvennom Pitanii*. Moscow: Gostorgizdat, 1959.

Statisticheskoe Upravlenie. Chuvashskoi ASSR, *Narodnoe Khoziaistvo Chuvashskoi ASSR*. Cheboksary, Chuvashskoe Gosudarstvennoe Izdatel'stvo, 1957 [a].

————. Goroda Leningrada, *Narodnoe Khoziaistvo Goroda Leningrada*. Moscow: Gosstatizdat, 1957 [b].

————. Goroda Moskvy, *Moskva, Razvitie Khoziaistva i Kul'tury Goroda*. Moscow: Moskovskii Rabochii, 1958.

Stewart, P. W., and Dewhurst, J. F. *Does Distribution Cost Too Much?* New York: The Twentieth Century Fund, 1939.

Tawney, R. H. *Religion and the Rise of Capitalism*. New York: Harcourt, Brace and World, 1926.

Tenenbaum, M. "O Vyborochnykh Obsledovaniiakh v Statistike Sovetskoi Torgovii," *Vestnik Statistiki*, No. 3, 1954.

Titel'baum, N. P. *Statistika Sovetskoi Torgovli*. Moscow: Gosstatizdat, 1955.

Tiukov, V. S. *Sovetskaia Torgovlia v Semiletke*. Moscow: Znanie, 1959.

————. "Zadachi Ukrepleniia Khoziaistvennogo Rascheta

v Sovetskoi Torgovle," *Sovetskaia Torgovlia,* May, 1954.

Tovarvi Slovar', Vols. I–VIII. Moscow: Gostorgizdat, 1956–59.

Trakhtenberg, G. L., and Sablina, T. N. *Metody Izucheniia Pokupatel'skogo Sprosa na Promyshlennye Tovary.* Moscow: Gostorgizdat, 1957.

Tsagolov, H. A. (ed.). *Zakon Stoimosti i Ego Rol' pri Sotsializme.* Moscow: Gosplanizdat, 1959.

Tsentral'noe Statisticheskoe Upravlenie. *Narodnoe Khoziaistvo SSSR.* Moscow: Gosstatizdat, 1956 (TsSU 1).

————. *Narodnoe Khoziaistvo SSSR v 1956 Godu.* Moscow: Gosstatizdat, 1957 (TsSU 2).

————. *v 1958 Godu. Ibid.,* 1959 (TsSU 3).

————. *v 1959 Godu. Ibid.,* 1960 (TsSU 4).

————. *v 1960 Godu. Ibid.,* 1961 (TsSU 5).

————. *Sovetskaia Torgovlia.* Moscow: Gosstatizdat, 1956 (TsSU 6).

————. *Sovetskaia Torgovlia v RSFSR.* Moscow: Gosstatizdat, 1958 (TsSU 7).

————. *SSSR v Tsifrakh.* Moscow: Gosstatizdat, 1958 (TsSU 8).

————. *SSSR v Tsifrakh v 1959 Godu.* Moscow: Gosstatizdat, 1960 (TsSU 9).

————. *SSSR v Tsifrakh v 1960 Godu.* 1961 (TsSU 10).

————. *Narodnoe Khoziaistvo Moskovskoi Oblasti.* Moscow: Moskovskii Rabochii, 1958 (TsSU 11).

————. *Dostizheniia Sovetskoi Belorussii za 50 Let.* Minsk: Gosstatizdat, 1958 (TsSU 12).

————. *SSSR v Tsifrakh v 1961 Godu.* Moscow: Gosstatizdat, 1962 (TsSU 13).

Tsymbal, G. "Utochnit' Klassifikatsiiu Oshovykh Fundov v Torgovle," *Sovetskaia Torgovlia,* October, 1958.

United States Bureau of the Census. *Statistical Abstract of the United States: 1959.* Washington, D.C.: Government Printing Office, 1959.

Ushakov, V. *Kreditovanie Torgovykh Organizatsii.* Moscow: Gosfinizdat, 1956.

Usokin, M. M. *Organizatsiia i Planirovanie Kratkosroch-nogo Kredita* (2nd ed.). Moscow: Gosfinizdat, 1956.

Vasilenko, T., and Sushko, A. "Protiv Izlishnikh Zven'ev v Optovoi Torgovle," *Sovetskaia Torgovlia,* June, 1959.

Vasil'ev, S. S., Kulikov, A. G., and Smotrina, N. A. *Tovarnye Fondy Trud Kadry i Zarabotnaia Plata Izderzskhi Obrashcheniia v Sovetskoi Torgovle.* Moscow: Gostorgizdat, 1958.

Vasil'ev, V. V. *Sovetskaia Torgovaia Reklama.* Moscow: Gostorgizdat, 1951.

Vinogradov, V. I., and Kaminskii, Ia. A. *Organizatsiia i Tekhnika Sovetskoi. Torgovli.* Moscow: Gostorgizdat, 1954.

Voloshnikov, A. T., Litvinshenko, P. S., and Shutov, I. N. *Peredovoi Kolkhoznyi Rynok.* Moscow: Gostorgizdat, 1958.

Ware, Henry. "Costs of Distribution in Soviet Domestic Trade," *Journal of Marketing,* July, 1950 [a].

————. "The Procurement Problem in Soviet Retail Trade," *Journal of Marketing,* October, 1950 [b].

Zaslavskii, A. P. *Izuchenie Sprosa Pokupatelei v Moskovskoi Tsentralnom Univermage.* Moscow: Gostorgizdat, 1957.

Zlobin, I. *Sushchnost' i Funktsii Deneg v SSSR.* Moscow: Gosfinizdat, 1956.
Zverev, A. G. *Finansy i Sotsialisticheskoe Stroitel'stvo.* Moscow: Gosfinizdat, 1957.
————. *Voprosy Natsional'nogo Dokhoda i Finansov SSSR.* Moscow: Gosfinizdat, 1958.

PERIODICALS

American Economic Review
Bol'shevik
Current Digest of the Soviet Press
Den'gi i Kredit
Ekonomicheskaia Gazeta
Finansy SSSR
Izvestiia (journal)
Izvestiia (newspaper)
Journal of Marketing
Journal of Political Economy
Kazakhstanskaia Pravda
Kommunist (journal)
Kommunist (newspaper)
Kommunist Tadzhikistana
New York Times
Novye Tovary
Planovoe Khoziaistvo
Pravda
Printer's Ink

Problems of Communism
Problems of Economics
Review of Economic Studies
Sovetskaia Belorussia
Sovetskaia Estoniia
Sovetskaia Kirgiziia
Sovetskaia Latviia
Sovetskaia Litva
Sovetskaia Moldavia
Sovetskaia Rossiia
Sovetskaia Torgovlia (journal)
Sovetskaia Torgovlia (newspaper)
Turkmenskaia Iskra
Vestnik Moskovskogo Universiteta
Vestnik Statistiki
Voprosy Ekonomiki
Wall Street Journal
Zariia Vostoka

MISCELLANEOUS

Goldman, Marshall I. *Travel Notes, July 1959.* Mimeographed, Russian Research Center, Harvard University, 1960.

Hunter, Holland. *Notes on Another Trip to the USSR.* Mimeographed, Haverford College, January, 1960.

Report of the American Marketing Delegation to the Soviet Union. Mimeographed, Harvard Business School, 1960.

INDEX

Acceptance, 118-125

Accounting, 22, 23, 24, 152, 155, 165-166, 207
  see also Capital; Credit; Install-ment credit; Interest; Profit; Turnover taxes

Accreditation, 118-125

Advertising, 2, 3, 24, 26-28, 48, 79-80, 103, 152, 160-166, 176, 183, 188, 194, 195-197, 199-201

Agriculture, 43

Bankruptcy (*see* Loss)

Bergson, Abram, 178n

Bespalov, M., 58n, 135-136

Black market, 89

Book stores, 16

Budget studies, 52-56, 72-76

Bureau for Reciprocal Accounting, 119

Bureaucracy, 28, 38, 103, 129-149

Buyer, 22, 59-60
  see also Tovarovedy

Capital, 111-117, 161, 182
  see also Credit; Installment credit; Interest; Profit; Turn-over taxes

Cash, 107-108, 116-117

Catholic Church, 2

Central Statistical Administration (TsSU), 53-54, 72

Channels of distribution, 10-11, 30, 31, 33, 34, 39, 61, 77, 188-189, 205

City planning, 66-69

Collective farm market (*see* Kol-khoz market)

Commission trade
  food, 39, 43-44, 50, 188
  manufactured goods, 16-17
  sales volume, 12, 44

Contracts, 56-57, 59-60, 78
  see also Ordering and allocation

Control by the ruble, 116
  see also Capital; Credit; Install-ment credit; Interest; Profit; Turnover taxes

Cooperative trade network, 11, 25, 34-44, 49-50, 54, 58, 88-91, 113, 124n, 164, 165, 167, 169-171, 189, 204-205
  administrative and structural or-ganization, 34-44
  sales volume, 12, 46

Costs of distribution, 3, 84, 100, 109-111, 151-179, 182-183, 187, 190-191, 201
  American, 152-153, 155-157, 160-168, 171-174, 176-179, 182
  restaurants, 154, 167, 169, 170-172
  retail, 151-179
  wholesale, 153-157, 167-168, 174-175

Council of Ministers, 29-31, 33,

37, 40, 58-59, 96, 99, 100, 131, 141

Credit
long-term, 113-117, 161-163
short-term, 103, 113-128, 151, 161-163, 183
see also Capital; Installment credit; Interest; Profit; Turnover taxes

Demand, 57, 71, 74, 83, 86-95, 97, 102, 104-105, 136, 191-192
elasticity, 71-72, 74, 90, 192
estimation, 52-57, 65-66, 71-77, 80-81, 192-193
Department stores, 13-14, 35, 161-162, 193, 196, 197
Depreciation, 115
Detskii Mir, 13, 68
Director's Fund, 115
Discretionary income, 72, 192, 196
Dom Modelei (style centers), 56
Drug stores, 16, 164

Employees (see Salesclerks; Wages)
England, Wilbur B., 161-162

Fefilov, A., 163n
Finance (see Capital; Credit; Installment credit; Interest; Profit; Turnover taxes)
Frederick Engels Institute, 26
Functions of marketing, 2-5, 8-9, 32-34, 201, 205, 207
Funded goods, 32, 57-59, 78, 80

Gerschenkron, Alexander, 146n
Glut, on market, 69-74, 79-80, 91, 94, 191, 193-195, 198-202
see also Inventory
Gogol', B. I., 66
Gosbank, 54, 107, 113-128
Gosplan, 25, 31-33, 53-54, 58-59, 78, 96, 99, 135, 190, 206
Government revenue, 86-87, 90
Government store network, 11-17, 44, 46, 58, 89-90

administrative and structural organization, 20-34, 40-41, 44, 49-50, 58-59, 96, 99, 189-190, 204-207
sales volume, 12, 46
see also Ministry of Trade
Grocery store, 15
GUM (Glavnyi Universalnyi Magazin), 13, 14, 196

Holzman, Franklyn, 88, 90
Honesty, 89, 129-132, 139, 144, 146-147
Hubbard, Leonard E., 203, 205

Iarmarki (see Trade fair)
Incentives, 124-130, 143-148
India, 177n, 201
Industrial production (see Planning, industry)
Inflation, 87-90, 105, 126n, 204
Installment credit, 162, 183, 188, 194, 197-198, 200
see also Capital; Credit; Interest; Profit; Turnover taxes
Interest, 103-104, 114, 158-163, 165, 183, 195
see also Capital; Credit; Installment credit; Profit; Turnover taxes
Inventory, 55-56, 73, 80, 87, 94, 103, 105, 113-114, 120, 145, 148, 161-162, 183, 192-193, 195
Isaacson, H. Lawrence, 161

Kaplan, Norman, 179
Kassa, 17-18, 132-133
Kerblay, Basile, 48n
Khozraschet (financial accounting), 108-111
Khrushchev, Nikita S., 73, 76
Kolkhoz (collective farm) market, 12, 42-48, 50, 54, 87-90, 153, 167-175, 204
Konius, A. A., 71n
Korolev, D. D., 199-200

Korzhenevskii, I., 72, 76

Location, 54-55, 56, 66-69, 137,
    177-178, 183
    see also Cooperative trade net-
    work; Government store net-
    work
Loss, 108, 125-128, 139

McNair, Malcolm P., 161
Mail order, 19-20, 23, 35-36, 39,
    190, 194
Margin, 107-111, 138, 153, 155-
    156, 166-171
Markdown, 94-95, 194-195
Market research, 22, 26, 70-77,
    148, 193, 201-202
    see also Budget studies; De-
    mand, estimation
Markup (see Margin; Rebates)
Marshall, Alfred, 102
Marx, Karl
    attitude toward marketing, 2-4,
    185, 187-189, 191, 196, 200-
    202
    Marxism and pricing, 84, 86,
    101-105, 195
Material responsibility, 132-134,
    139, 147
Mikoyan, A., 195
Ministry of Finance, 96, 120-121,
    127
Ministry of Trade, 15-17, 23-26,
    28-33, 40-41, 50, 53, 58-59,
    77-78, 96, 99, 107, 111-112,
    116, 127-128, 134, 141-142,
    145, 164, 169-170, 186, 190,
    195, 199, 206-207

NEP (New Economic Policy),
    203-204
Newspaper stands, 16, 164
NITTOP, 24, 26, 77

Ordering and allocation, 52, 55-
    62, 69-70, 77-81

Organization of trade network,
    10-11, 58-62, 78, 189-190
    see also Cooperative trade net-
    work; Government store net-
    work; Kolkhoz market
ORS (Workers Supply Depart-
    ments), 15-16, 164, 169-170

Pavlov, Dmitri, 29
Pawnshops, 16
Planning
    distribution, 51-52, 57-62, 65,
    69-81, 110-111, 125, 127-128,
    134-139, 191-193, 198-202
    finance, 107-128, 134-139
    industry, 51-52, 57, 59-61, 63-
    66, 71, 78, 79, 125, 128, 134-
    136, 191-193, 198-202
Plekhanov Institute, 24, 26
Posyltorg (see Mail order)
Prices, 24, 31-32, 37, 58n, 83-105,
    191, 193-196, 199, 200-201
    cooperative trade, 37, 88-90
    determination of, 31-32, 96-101,
    109-111
    Kolkhoz market, 47-48, 87-90
    subsidy, 93
    zones, 31-32, 91-93, 97, 99-100,
    109-110
Producer's cooperatives, 42, 44
Product differentiation, 188, 189,
    194, 196-197
Productivity, 176-183, 190, 201
Profit, 84-86, 101, 104-105, 107-
    109, 111-112, 115-116, 120,
    125-127, 135, 138, 153, 167-
    171
    see also Capital; Credit; Install-
    ment credit; Interest; Turn-
    over taxes

Quality, 24, 66, 124-125, 136-139,
    145-146, 196-197

Rabochii mest (see Salesclerks)
RAND Corporation, 179

Rationing, 204-205

Rebates *(skidki)*, 85, 96-97, 109-111, 120-122, 137-138

Rent, 103-104, 158-162

Restaurants, 15, 17, 23, 26, 34, 37, 39, 107, 110, 133-134, 145
   costs of distribution, 154, 167, 169, 170-171

Retailing
   costs of distribution, 151-176
   location, 10-17, 66-69, 137
   in rural areas *(see* Cooperative trade network)
   in urban areas *(see* Government store network)
   see also Kolkhoz market

Rochdale cooperatives, 36, 37

Romanov, A., 76n

Rynochnyi fond (see Funded goods)

Salesclerks, 17-20, 68, 80, 132-133, 147, 178-182

Scholastics, 2-4

Secondhand stores, 16

Self-service, 18-19, 133, 147, 190, 197

Service, 137, 145-149, 155, 176-183

Shopping centers, 68

Shopping procedure, 17-20, 132-133

Shortages, 57-58, 62-66, 69-70, 87-91, 189-191

Smirnov, A., 32, 58n

Sobolev, A. I., 74

Soiuzglavtorg, 31-33, 58n, 59, 78, 135, 206

Sovnarkhozy (regional economic councils), 25, 29, 31, 33, 53, 58, 62, 99

Standard of living, 69-76, 87, 146-148, 189, 191-194

Stepaniants, T. S., 26-27, 163, 196
   see also Advertising

Store network and outlets *(see* Cooperative trade network; Government store network; Location)

Storming, 125

Stroibank, 115
   see also Capital; Credit; Installment credit; Interest; Profit; Turnover taxes

Style, 56, 75, 135-136, 192-193

Surplus value, 86, 101-105

Taxes, 37, 120
   see also Government revenue; Turnover taxes

Tiukov, V., 32

Tolkachi, 142

Torg (trade organization), 22-25, 48, 55, 59-61, 66, 111, 115
   see also Ministry of Trade

Torgbank, 115

Torgreklama, 24, 26-27, 163, 196
   see also Advertising

Tovarovedy (department managers) 20, 22, 59-60

Trade fair, 24, 79-80, 188, 194, 198-199

Transportation, 2, 3, 24, 37, 48, 56, 97, 109, 156-158, 162, 165, 207

Tsentralsoiuz (see Cooperative trade network)

TsSU *(see* Central Statistical Administration)

TsUM (Central Department Store), 13, 145, 196

Turnover taxes, 84-91, 93, 104-105, 116, 120, 153, 167-168, 171-174
   see also Capital; Credit; Installment credit; Interest; Profit

Udarnik, 145n

Upravlenie (Administration) *(see* Ministry of Trade)

Vending machines, 20, 190

Wages, 24, 39, 75, 116, 119-120, 143-145, 158-159, 162, 165-166, 182

Wainstein, Eleanor, 179

War, 86-87, 204

Warehouse (*sklad* or *bax*), 2, 3, 22-23, 25, 39, 40, 60-61, 102, 103, 109, 157

Wholesale, 10-11, 22-25, 32, 34, 38-41, 60-62, 78-80, 85, 108-109, 111, 118-120, 122-123, 138, 148, 188-190, 198, 201, 205, 207

costs of distribution, 153-157, 165, 167-168, 174-175

Workers Supply Departments (*see* ORS)

Zaiavki and *Zakazy* (*see* Ordering and allocation)

Zoning laws, 67